# You Can *Free Yourself* from Alcohol &Drugs

*Work a Program*
*That Keeps You in Charge*

Doug Althauser, M.Ed., CSAC, MAC

New Harbinger Publications

## Publisher's Note

*This publication is designed to provide accurate and authoritative information in regard to the subject matter covered. It is sold with the understanding that the publisher is not engaged in rendering psychological, financial, legal, or other professional services. If expert assistance or counseling is needed, the services of a competent professional should be sought.*

Distributed in the U.S.A. by Publishers Group West; in Canada by Raincoast Books; in Great Britain by Airlift Book Company, Ltd.; in South Africa by Real Books, Ltd.; in Australia by Boobook; and in New Zealand by Tandem Press.

Copyright © 1998 by Doug Althauser, M.Ed., CSAC, MAC
New Harbinger Publications, Inc.
5674 Shattuck Avenue
Oakland, CA 94609

Cover design © 1998 by Lightbourne Images
Edited by Catharine Sutker
Text design by Tracy Marie Powell

Library of Congress Catalog Card Number: 98-66699
ISBN 1-57224-118-7 Paperback

All Rights Reserved

Printed in United States of America on recycled paper

New Harbinger Publications' Website address: www.newharbinger.com

First printing

*To Sandy*

# Contents

# Acknowledgments

I believe that life is best pursued as a group event, not an individual endeavor. Writing this book has been a study in that belief. I don't think I could have accomplished this without the aid of many people, all of whom have been sources of support for me.

I began the actual outline of this book in October of '92. In May of the next year I conducted a short workshop to get feedback on the ideas and the vocabulary I was using to explain my ideas. My thanks to Sandy Riebow, Alan Lubliner, Candyce Ka'aiai, Tom Ruble, Jo-Ann Adams, Paul Ferrin, and Diane Lierman for attending that workshop. They helped me begin the process of editing myself.

Thanks to those who read the first draft of this book and gave me their opinions: Tom Metz, Lindsay Fox, Allan Mossing, Sandy (again), Heather Cattell, and my mother, Martha Althauser. I also need to thank my father here, Tom. All their feedback helped me make major revisions.

I also thank the therapists who have helped me turn these ideas into two successful treatment programs for Kaiser Permanente in Hawaii: Sandy, yet again, Maxine Martinie, Belle Chung,

Marlene Nalani, Bob McClay, Marianne Gordon-Ringberg, Monika Vassallo, David Fukuzawa, Varna Nakihei, Sam Alfapada, Patti Tada, Peggy Van Cleve, Janis Cierie, Jim Lovett, Chandra Smith, Cynthia Greene, Benjamin Kaneaiakala, Kaori Watanabe, William Mouser, and Elaine Maher. These therapists helped fine-tune the treatment concepts into a verifiably effective professional program of recovery. Thanks to Bonnie Reilly, CNS, Clinic Manager and my supervisor at the Department of Mental Health Services, and Marvin Matthews, M.D., Chief of the Department. Both trusted my ideas and have supported my work.

I am in debt also to those patients with whom I have worked using this treatment approach. They have overcome their dependencies and have improved their lives. As they learned how to recover, they helped me understand how to present the recovery process to others so they could learn how as well. A big part of this book is the result of their successes.

I have presented more workshops to present my ideas to yet more colleagues. The comments I received from the participants, and their stories of success with using this approach helped me craft this finished version. Their enthusiasm, which has continued well past those workshops, has also been fuel for my efforts.

Thanks to those people all around the country who gave me feedback as I was rewriting: Liz Lottes, Karen Hunsaker, Linda Lewis, Josef Steiff, Theresa Riedman, and several anonymous people I bumped into along the way and who asked me about this work on planes, on vacation, or in restaurants. Their comments gave me to believe I was working on something of value.

Thanks for the support I have received from everyone at New Harbinger Publications. Their support helped me turn my ideas into a book that was clearer than I could have written completely on my own.

It's funny sometimes to recollect how life placed before me so many people who were interested in these ideas and willing to talk about them with me. I don't believe in coincidences; I believe these people were carefully (and thankfully) placed in my path by my ultimate source of support, who I choose to call God.

I will repeat one last thank you to Sandy Riebow, who helped me with this project from the very beginning. Practically speaking, she gave me encouragement, feedback, direction, reality checks, and a better understanding of some of the points from AA and the Big Book that I wasn't quite getting. Speaking from the

heart, the friendship I experience with her (and her husband, Daniel) has given me the main source of my stamina as I worked to finish this book and fulfill a dream of mine. Dedicating this book to her is but a token of the debt of gratitude I believe I owe her.

# Introduction

This book will give you all the tools you need to free yourself from alcohol and drugs. First, you will determine whether or not you actually have chemical dependency. If you feel that you do, the ten goals in this book will help you to overcome your chemical dependency. Furthermore, this process will let you keep yourself in charge of your recovery while you do it.

The process in this book uses research which shows how people recover best from drug addictions and alcohol dependency. The research is applied to one of the oldest and most effective strategies for recovery. The following information about the process offers some tips on how you can get the most out of your recovery program.

## A Little Bit of History

Beginning in the 1930s and for nearly four decades, the standard for treatment and recovery from chemical dependency was Twelve-Step programs like Alcoholics Anonymous (AA) and Narcotics Anonymous (NA). Twelve-Step programs provide a spiritual blueprint for recovery. In a nutshell, members identify their own God, then rely on the support and guidance of their God and of other group members to help them become sober and stay that way. The programs were effective—many addicts and alcoholics got better by using them. Today, Twelve-Step programs are still more prevalent than other recovery programs.

In the 1970s, the culture of North America changed. People became less likely to discuss God or spirituality in informal group settings like AA or NA meetings. Furthermore, people began to express pride over their individual characteristics, like their culture, their gender, race, ethnicity, or personal philosophy.

This independence made it tough for a lot of addicts and alcoholics to accept the spiritual philosophy of Twelve-Step programs. Not surprisingly, chemically dependent people began to ask for alternatives to the Twelve Steps. As a result, three different groups began on a national level helping people to recover: Women For Sobriety, Secular Organizations for Sobriety (or Save Our Selves), and Rational Recovery. These groups provided an alternative to Twelve-Step programs. More importantly, these alternative programs worked. Meanwhile, a behavior-modification program run by the Schick-Shadel Institute, which began before AA, has continued to operate, helping problem drinkers become sober and maintain sobriety.

A few other strategies for recovery have proven effective for people wishing to overcome their chemical dependency. Some have found religion to be an effective tool to help them become and remain drug- or alcohol-free. These people must obey the rules of their church and stick with other members of their faith. Others have found that strictly following the rules of their culture have helped them stay sober. Again, these people must obey the rules of their tribe, community, or culture, and respect their peers.

## What Recovery History Shows

All these recovery strategies—that is, Twelve-Step programs, the three other kinds of self-help groups, Schick Shadel, religious influences, and cultural influences—require people to do three things. Take note, because if you want to free yourself of alcohol or drugs, you will have to do the following three things too.

- Stay away from drugs and alcohol *forever*.

- Change your lifestyle to help you stay away from drugs and alcohol as well as the opportunity to even be *around* drugs or alcohol in unwise ways.

- Get help from a support group, or from some kind of a group of people who can help you *stay drug-* and *alcohol-free.*

The approach to recovery described in this book will help you do these three things. The ten goals that make up the process in this book come from the *therapeutic,* that is, the nonspiritual recovery concepts found in the Twelve Steps.

# Why Use the Concepts from the Twelve Steps?

You might wonder why a new, nonspiritual recovery process would be based on an established spiritual program like the Twelve Steps. The answer has two parts.

First, the Twelve Steps have been around for sixty years and have helped many people recover from chemical dependency. There are more Twelve-Step programs around than any other treatment program. You can probably find an AA or NA support meeting easier than any other group.

Second, even if you choose not to go to a Twelve-Step meeting, the fact is that there are important concepts in each of the Twelve Steps that can help anyone who wants to recover from chemical dependency. This book uses those concepts and gives you the tools to use in your own life and recovery. You don't have to be a member of AA or NA to use this approach.

The program in this book is based on a program already proven to be effective; however, it only uses the parts that work for everyone.

It is strictly *therapeutic* and *individualized.* You will be given a blueprint for recovery. You'll use that blueprint the way you want to, according to what makes you comfortable. Your program of recovery won't look exactly like anyone else's. That's okay, as long as the program you set up works for you.

If you want to make your program spiritual, then do that. If you don't, that's fine too. Or if you want to rely on a certain type of group, then do that. Your program can include particular activities, people, or other things if that's what you want. You can make this program into anything you want it to be, with only one rule: *Anything you do with this blueprint has to help you stay away from drugs and alcohol.*

As mentioned, the process of recovery in this book is based upon the therapeutic concepts found in the Twelve Steps. However, don't think that this process is a Twelve-Step program. Also, don't think that this process has anything to do with Alcoholics Anonymous, Narcotics Anonymous, or any other Twelve-Step program.

This process is not aligned with any Twelve-Step program at all. AA did not ask for this book to be written. AA did give permission to use the steps in this book; because AA holds the copyright to the steps it was necessary to request such permission.

Here are the Twelve Steps, which will be discussed in the next ten chapters of this book.

1. We admitted we were powerless over alcohol—that our lives had become unmanageable.

2. Came to believe that a Power greater than ourselves could restore us to sanity.

3. Made a decision to turn our will and our lives over to the care of God *as we understood Him.*

4. Made a searching and fearless moral inventory of ourselves.

5. Admitted to God, to ourselves, and to another human being the exact nature of our wrongs.

6. Were entirely ready to have God remove all these defects of character.

7. Humbly asked Him to remove our shortcomings.

8. Made a list of all persons we had harmed, and became willing to make amends to them all.

9. Made direct amends to such people wherever possible, except when to do so would injure them or others.

10. Continued to take personal inventory and when we were wrong promptly admitted it.

11. Sought through prayer and meditation to improve our conscious contact with God, *as we understood Him*, praying only for knowledge of His will for us and the power to carry that out.

12. Having had a spiritual awakening as the result of these steps, we tried to carry this message to alcoholics, and to practice these principles in all our affairs.

The Twelve Steps are reprinted with permission of Alcoholics Anonymous World Services, Inc. Permission to reprint the Twelve Steps does not mean that AA has reviewed or approved the contents of this publication, nor that AA agrees with the views expressed herein. AA is a program of recovery from alcoholism *only*—use of the Twelve Steps in connection with programs and activities that are patterned after AA, but that address other problems, or in any other non-AA context, does not imply otherwise.

# How to Use This Book

Here are some pointers on how you can get the most out of this book.

## *Do the Goals in Order*

The ten goals in this book build upon each other in their order. You should finish the first goal before going on to the second, and so on. Each goal relies on you understanding the previous goals. If you skip ahead, this process won't make sense to you and you won't get any help from it. So, don't skip ahead; work on these goals in order.

## *Be Prepared to Write*

You will have ten separate assignments that will require you to do some writing, mostly making lists. As you complete the goals, it's important to write down the answers to your assignments.

This is important because throughout this book and your goal-work, you'll refer back to the work you've already done. Don't rely on your memory at those times. Writing down the work you do on your assignments will give you something to look back over as you progress. Your recovery will be stronger for it.

You could write your assignments directly in this book. If you have a journal, you could complete your assignments in your journal. If you don't have a journal, now would be a good time to start one. Don't worry about anyone grading your spelling or grammar. If you feel that you are not a strong writer, then use a tape recorder or have someone else write while you dictate.

## You're in Charge, but Recognize Your Limits

You get to use this program to tailor your recovery to meet your own individual needs. But keep in mind you may not always be the best person to recognize when you could use more help. If you could have taken care of your problem all by yourself, you would've done so before you began to read this book. You'll need some support, some outside help. Don't hesitate to find it. The up-coming chapters will give you more tips on how to find that help.

## Don't Delay Your Recovery

This process is designed to help you find your own way to recovery quickly. Once you get started, you should be able to reach goal six within a short time—probably in less than two weeks. You should be up to goal eight within a month from your start date. After that, you'll maintain your recovery with the last goals for a long time.

If the process is taking you longer than this, then you're having problems. Either you're not really committed to recovery, or you're finding recovery too confusing to accept. In either case, get some outside help. Find a professional who is familiar with recovery, who can help you figure things out. Or find a supportive non-professional who can help you understand what you need to do to recover.

*Don't delay your recovery.* Every day that you do something to slow your pace is a day you might relapse and start to use drugs or alcohol again.

## Your Recovery Process

First, you'll need to figure out whether or not you really do have chemical dependency. You'll identify this in the first chapter. Next, in chapters 2 through 10, you'll work on the process of recovery. Chapter 11 will give you some more pointers on making your recovery successful. Chapter 12 is written for therapists who would use this process to treat chemically dependent patients. Chapter 13 provides resources for support which you can use to help your recovery.

Each of the first ten chapters looks at one or two of the Twelve Steps. Certain words within each step are identified as being important therapeutic concepts for recovery. Sometimes, the therapeutic concepts within each step get examined according to how the words were defined when the Twelve Steps were first written. The definitions of the words from the Twelve Steps in this book come from *The New Century Dictionary*, which was published when the Twelve Steps were written.

The concepts from the steps are rewritten into a therapeutic plan which, if you follow it, will help you become and stay free of alcohol and drugs. If you use the plan as suggested in this book, you'll overcome chemical dependency.

*Now, turn the page and get started.*

# 1

## Make a
## Self-Diagnosis

Do you believe you have alcohol dependency or an addiction to drugs? Would you rather use another name for it, like alcoholism, or being a drunk, or a druggie? Do you not understand why other people say you have chemical dependency? You can answer these questions by making a self-diagnosis with the following information. Your first goal is to make a self-diagnosis.

## Why Do You Need A
## Self-Diagnosis?

If you don't believe you have chemical dependency, you won't be willing to treat yourself for chemical dependency. It's this simple: You need a self-diagnosis to help you understand why you need to treat yourself.

Treating your chemical dependency is challenging. You won't want to go through with it if you don't believe you need to do it. If you don't diagnose *yourself* with chemical dependency, then you won't follow the advice of any treatment program. Making a self-diagnosis also puts you in charge of your recovery from the very start. If you can understand how it is that you have chemical dependency, you'll be more willing to commit to the work of recovery.

## Denial or Skepticism?

There is such a thing as healthy skepticism. However, there's a major difference between this and denial. If you don't think you have chemical dependency, perhaps you think you're just a healthy skeptic. After all, you might tell yourself, who knows you and your health better than you? For example, suppose a physician diagnosed you—you being a woman—with recurrent epididymitis. The doctor said she could tell you had it just by the way you were sitting. What if when you asked why, and what does "epididymitis" mean, the doctor told you not to ask questions. She was the expert, and her word should be enough. Now, would you want treatment without understanding the condition? Probably not.

Or, suppose a doctor diagnosed you—you being a man—with vaginismus. You probably would've wanted explanations and proof. You'd have wanted to know how the doctor could tell that. Maybe you wanted to know why the doctor even mentioned it considering you'd gone to the doctor's office with an entirely different problem. Would you treat your vaginismus based on these vague conclusions? Probably not.

If you were in either of these situations, you should ask for explanations and even second opinions. Hopefully, you would try to learn as much as you could about epididymitis or vaginismus until you felt certain you knew what the terms meant. You would keep learning until you understood why you had those problems and were satisfied that the diagnosis really does name what you had.

In these examples, your skepticism would be very healthy for you. After all, no woman can have epididymitis; and no man can have vaginismus. You would want to know these facts before your doctor prescribed treatments for those problems! You should ask for details whenever anyone else is trying to tell you something about your health. Don't just take their word for it, figure it out for yourself; make a self-diagnosis. That's the healthy, skeptical thing to do.

On the other hand, if you don't think you have chemical dependency, your disbelief could show that you're in an unhealthy state of denial. Most chemically dependent people experience this. Denial means that even though you have chemical dependency, you may refuse to believe it, or to take an honest look at your problem. If you're in denial, you won't want to learn more about it because then you might have to do something about it. You might resent someone else's diagnosis of you because their opinion seems more like an attack against you rather than a believable diagnosis. You might also realize how much work you'll have to do to treat it, making you not want to face up to it.

These are examples of unhealthy reasons to deny that you have chemical dependency. An honest denial of your potential problem can come only after looking at all your symptoms, and then truthfully concluding that you really don't have chemical dependency.

Be honest—make a self-diagnosis. Work through this goal. If you don't have chemical dependency, then you don't have it. If you do, you need to do something about it.

# What Is Chemical Dependency?

Chemical dependency has three basic symptoms. If you have chemical dependency that means the following are true:

1. When you choose to use drugs or alcohol, you cannot always predict how much you will use.

2. You cannot always predict what will happen when you use drugs or alcohol.

3. This is a permanent problem, not a temporary one.

Chemical dependency is a permanent problem. When you use drugs or drink, you take away your ability for sound judgment. Without sound judgment, you cannot have a healthy lifestyle.

If you have chemical dependency, most likely your life has developed some problems. Your life doesn't have to involve one awful calamity after another for this to be true. However, when you use drugs or alcohol, you suffer problems that you feel you have no ability to control.

For example, your relationship with your family or friends may have suffered due to things you did while using drugs or alcohol. Maybe they're not talking to you these days; or maybe you wish they wouldn't talk to you so much. You might have problems related to the amount of money you've spent on drugs or alcohol. Now you owe more than you can pay back. You might have caused some problems at your office because of what you had done while using drugs or alcohol. Perhaps your supervisor is eyeing your performance more these days than in your past. All this may have made you wonder whether or not you have a dependency to drugs or alcohol.

You might have spoken to professionals who have told you that you have chemical dependency. Perhaps you have read articles or heard reports that suggest that anyone with your symptoms has chemical dependency. You probably found all these opinions (especially the ones you never asked for) irritating, and unhelpful in determining whether or not you really have it.

## Losing Your Judgment

One of the deceptive qualities of chemical dependency is that your life may not seem catastrophic even though you do have a dependency. Most of the time, chemical dependency doesn't affect your life *constantly*. It's possible that you aren't necessarily experiencing problem after problem, hour upon hour, day after day. The fact that you don't have constant problems may help you deny that you have chemical dependency. You could easily say, "After all, I don't have a constant problem, my life isn't in ceaseless shambles, I must not have a *real* problem."

Maybe your life isn't a total disaster, but if you have chemical dependency, your problem is permanent even if it's not constant. Chemical dependency has this unexplainable characteristic—when it isn't *active*, that is, when you avoid using drugs or drinking alcohol, you don't experience obvious problems because of drugs or alcohol. When chemical dependency is active, however, you continue to want to use or drink in spite of whatever problems you might undergo. You may suffer enormous consequences, but you still want to use or drink. This is the result of losing your sound judgment.

At some point, you may have suffered a particular consequence that made you want to stop for good. So you stopped. Then, after the heat of the consequence died down, you began drinking or using again. Then, after a while, your problems began all over again.

First things first. Figure out if you have the problem before you start to work on the solution. Right now, you probably don't know how to figure out for sure if you do or do not have chemical dependency. Just pay careful attention to the following explanations, do the assignments, and you will figure it out.

# Don't Bite Off Too Much Too Soon

Here is a word of caution before you conclude whether or not you have chemical dependency: You might feel inclined to make a deep, emotional, analytical evaluation of yourself. You might want to think about your childhood traumas, troubled adolescence, war traumas, insecurities, your troubled marriage or former relationships and the intense feelings they have caused. **Well, don't.**

You don't need to go through an intense evaluation to make a self-diagnosis for chemical dependency. Thinking about all the traumatic events in your life may actually hinder you from making a self-diagnosis. Trying to figure out "why" you developed chemical dependency will not help you make a self-diagnosis or help you with your recovery. In the long run, evaluating your life may create anxiety, making you want to go use drugs or alcohol so you can find relief. You will have the chance to explore some personal issues when you work through the last three goals in this program. At that time, when you're enjoying being free of drugs or alcohol, you might discover some insights about the many things on which you blame your drug or alcohol use. However, right now, just focus on figuring out whether or not you do, in fact, have chemical dependency. Once you know that for sure, you can begin work to end it.

# The Concepts Behind Your Self-Diagnosis

This first goal comes from the first step of Alcoholics Anonymous, which helps members of AA figure out whether or not they have alcoholism. The work you do on this goal sets the stage for the rest of your recovery. In AA and NA, the first step helps chemically dependent people understand the nature of the problem of alcoholism or addiction. The first step reads "We admitted we *were powerless* over alcohol, that our lives had become *unmanageable.*" Note that even though this step mentions only alcohol, the concepts within this step will apply if you have a problem with alcohol or any other drug.

There are three important concepts from the first step that help explain the work of your first goal. These concepts are represented by the words *powerless*, *unmanageable*, and *were*. Each concept relates to one of those three basic symptoms of chemical dependency mentioned a few pages ago. Understanding these concepts will help you look for the symptoms that will help you make a self-diagnosis.

You may not like the words *powerless* and *unmanageable,* or feel humiliated about having to admit powerlessness or unmanageability over anything. But take a closer look at just what these words mean.

## *Powerlessness—A Symptom of Chemical Dependency*

When you're *powerless* over something, you can't control or predict it. For the purposes of this recovery process, powerlessness doesn't mean that you can't control anything in your life. The concept of powerlessness only has to do with whether or not you can control or predict your use of drugs or alcohol when you use or drink.

Powerlessness means that when you choose to use alcohol or drugs, you cannot always tell how much you will use or drink. That is all. To start the process of making a self-diagnosis, you need to figure out if you are powerless over your use of drugs or alcohol when you choose to use drugs or drink.

Do you want to argue that this concept has nothing to do with you? After all, you probably can sometimes control how much you will drink or use. However, powerless means you are unable to *consistently* predict your drinking or drug use. Yes you can, at times, limit your indulging; but can you control it *all the time*? If more often than not you drink more than you planned, or use more than you planned, then you've experienced powerlessness. Does this sound like you?

Signs of powerlessness usually have to do with the following

- Time

- Amount

- Money

That is, you can look for signs of your own powerlessness (and signs that you have this symptom of chemical dependency) by thinking about how much *time* you spend using your drug or alcohol, how *much* you use when you choose to use, or how much *money* you spend using your drug or alcohol. People who have chemical dependency cannot always predict these three things.

Does this sound familiar? Consider the following examples. Say you had your rent money in your pocket. On the way to your landlord you ran into an opportunity to score a lot of your favorite drug at a special price. Is there a chance you'd spend your rent on the drugs, and then try to talk your landlord into being patient for a while so you could scrounge up the rent again? If your answer is "yes," or "maybe," then this is a sign of powerlessness.

Or, suppose you promised to be home by 7 PM. Now it's 6:30 PM, you have twenty more minutes to drive home, but you decide to stop off at your favorite bar for a "quickie." Are you going to get home by 7? If your answer is "no," or "probably not," then this is a sign of powerlessness. What if you had a case of your favorite beer, frosty cold in the refrigerator, and you dared yourself to have just one can a day for twenty-four days, and no more than that, could you do it? How about this: If you had $400 worth of your favorite drug, and wanted to use only $100 tonight, saving the rest for the weekend, could you do that? If your answer to either of these is "no," or "hell no," then this is a sign of powerlessness.

## Thinking about Your Own Signs of Powerlessness

Answer the following questions about your own use of drugs or alcohol:

- Are there times when you spend more money on drugs or alcohol than you planned when you use or drink?

- Have you ever given yourself a limit (for example, $50), but then, as the night wore on, you spent more than your limit?

- Have you ever maxed-out a credit card because you were using drugs or alcohol?

- Have you ever gone to a bank's automatic teller machine several times in the same day or night to withdraw more money than you had planned?

- Have you ever borrowed money from people you shouldn't have in order to use drugs or drink (like friends, children, family members with a low income, or even loan sharks)?

- Have you ever spent money you shouldn't have on drugs or alcohol (like the rent money, your car payment, money for bills, or child-support payments)?

- Have you ever served your children or other family members unusual meals (like cold cereal for dinner, or junk food for breakfast) because you spent their food money on drugs or alcohol?

- Have you ever spent more time using drugs or alcohol than you had planned to spend?

- Have you ever missed an appointment because you were using or drinking?

- Have you ever shown up late to an appointment because of your use of drugs or alcohol?

- Have you ever blown off appointments, parties, dinner invitations, or dates because of your use of drugs or alcohol?

- Have you ever broken a promise to show up somewhere because you used drugs or drank?

- Have you ever chosen to miss family events because of your drug or alcohol use?

- Have you ever blown off spending holidays with your friends or family so that you could use drugs or drink alcohol?

- Have you ever used drugs or drank late into the night, or maybe all night, even though you knew you had to go to work or to school early the next morning?

- Have you ever used more of a drug or alcohol than you had planned to use?

- Have you ever told yourself that you were only going to use "*this* much," but then you actually used "*too* much"?

- Have you ever bought what you thought was enough drugs or alcohol to last you for a while, but then used it all at once?

- Have you ever bought drugs or alcohol for yourself and friends, but then pinched a little of their share for yourself before giving it to them?

- Have you ever bought drugs or alcohol for a few people, but then used it all before giving them their share?

- Have you ever tried to deal drugs, but ended up using all the supply before you could sell it?

- Have you ever told yourself you were going to use only a certain amount from now on, but then didn't keep your promise to yourself?

- Have you ever used so much of a drug that you ended up getting sick, or even wound up in an emergency room of a hospital, even though you weren't trying to hurt yourself?

How many questions did you answer "yes" to? Although there isn't a magic number that proves you have chemical dependency, if you answered "yes" to any or all of these questions it is a sign you're powerless over your drug or alcohol use. If you're powerless, you have one of the symptoms of chemical dependency. Having one symptom doesn't mean you have chemical dependency. Before you decide one way or the other about your self-diagnosis, think about the next concept of your self-diagnosis.

## Unmanageability—A Symptom of Chemical Dependency

When something is *unmanageable*, you cannot manage or handle the particular circumstance. Once again, this concept only refers to your life when you use drugs or alcohol. You lose the ability to manage or handle things when you use or drink—or, you can't predict what will happen in your life when you drink or use drugs. "But wait!" you now think, "My life isn't *completely* unmanageable."

Chemically dependent people's lives become unmanageable when they drink or use drugs. Although their lives probably seem fine, they still have chemical dependency. They may have nice families, hold down important jobs, and have no legal or financial problems. Nonetheless, when these people drink or use drugs, problems happen. These problems are things that might make chemical dependency easy for someone *else* to recognize. These are the family and relationship problems, financial troubles, work issues, legal difficulties, health concerns, and reputation-killers that all chemically dependent people experience. Of course, not everyone has a problem in every one of those categories, and some chemically dependent people's problems are more severe than those of others. These problems wouldn't have happened if they hadn't been using or drinking. Those problems are a sign of unmanageability and point to another symptom of chemical dependency.

If you have chemical dependency, you probably put some effort into making your problem not noticeable. Chemical dependency doesn't always live up to the popular idea of a devastating, publicly embarrassing, easily detectable pattern of behavior. Such a definition worked in the early days of AA, but today that definition is usually inaccurate. In the 1930s, a drinker needed to have "lost it all" before a doctor would diagnose alcoholism. Today, people of all ages and stages of life receive diagnoses of chemical dependency. Most dependent people have not suffered total devastation because of their problem.

You probably often enjoy your drinking or drug use. Maybe only some of your using or drinking results in unmanageable consequences. Those consequences, however, may affect a big part of your life. Your drinking or drug use can cause troubles for you with your family, work, friends, finances, reputation, health, or with the law. Consequences showing your unmanageability are things that wouldn't have happened if you hadn't used drugs or alcohol. Some examples of unmanageability are obvious: for example, you wouldn't get arrested for drunk driving if you hadn't been drinking; you couldn't be arrested for possession if you weren't in possession of drugs; an ex-lover wouldn't have blamed your drug use on the breakup if you hadn't used drugs; your boss wouldn't have fired you for a positive urine drug screen at work if you hadn't used drugs; or, you wouldn't have alcohol-related liver trouble if you hadn't drunk so much.

While the consequences just mentioned are pretty obvious signs of unmanageability, other consequences aren't so obvious. You may not have lost job opportunities if your drug use hadn't made you so unreliable. Your kids might have learned to be more confident if your drug use hadn't made you so untrustworthy. You might have kept more friendships if your drug use hadn't gotten in the way. You might have been able to retire earlier if you hadn't blown so much money on drugs or alcohol.

### Thinking about Your Own Signs of Unmanageability

Answer the following questions about your own use of drugs or alcohol:

- Have you noticed that, over the months or years, you have had to use more of your drug or alcohol in order to feel the effects the way you used to?

- Have you ever embarrassed yourself because of your drug or alcohol use?

- Have you ever disappointed yourself because you used or drank?

- Has your name ever been in the papers or on a news broadcast because of something that had to do with your drug or alcohol use?

- Does it ever disturb you that the way that you drink or use drugs goes against either the rules of your religion or your membership in a social group or civic organization?

- When you were using or drinking, have you ever neglected your responsibilities to your family, job, or finances?

- Have you ever been in trouble for the appointments you missed while you were using or drinking?

- Have you ever been in trouble because you broke a promise while you were drinking or using? Did you ever make a promise you shouldn't have made while you were drinking or using?

- Have you ever been arrested because of your drug or alcohol use?

- Have you ever had to go to jail because of something that had to do with your drug or alcohol use?

- Have you gone into debt because of your drug or alcohol use?

- Have you ever had to pay extra for something because of your drug or alcohol use? For example, have you had to pay higher insurance premiums because of your drinking or drug use?

- Have you ever had to pay for damages that were caused, one way or the other, by your drinking or drug use?

- Have you ever suffered some kind of health problem because of your drug use? For example, has your drug or alcohol use caused any trouble with your liver, skin, hair, or weight?

- Has a doctor or health professional ever told you that you should stop using or drinking?

- Have you ever hurt yourself while your were drinking or using? (Either by accident or on purpose?)

- Do you ever experience withdrawal symptoms? That is, does your body react to not having the drugs or alcohol?

- Do you get crankier when you go a few days without using or drinking?

- Do you have trouble sleeping when you don't use for a while?

- If you don't use or drink for a while, do you have odd dreams, or do you dream about using or drinking?

- Does your appetite change when you don't use or drink?

- Do you start to crave other kinds of drugs, or certain foods when you don't use or drink?

- Do you have muscle twitches or start to shake when you don't use or drink?

- While you use or drink, do you ever do things that you can't remember once you sober up?

- Have you had problems in your marriage that are the results of your drug or alcohol use?

- Has your family ever said they were concerned about your drug or alcohol use?

- Do you ever get upset with your family when they talk about your drinking or drug use?

- Do you think your family has lost their trust in you because of your drinking or drug use?

- Has your job performance suffered because of your drug or alcohol use?

- Have co-workers had to cover up for mistakes you have made because of your drinking or using?

- Have you been reprimanded at work because of something that had to do with drugs or alcohol (for example, tardiness, too much sick leave, or poor job performance)?

- Have you ever chosen a job that was beneath your abilities because you figured it would not interfere with your drug or alcohol use?

- Do your friends say they worry about your drug or alcohol use?

- Do you ever get upset when friends talk about your drug or alcohol use?

- Have you ever argued with your friends about your drug or alcohol use?

- Has your drug or alcohol use ever led to the end of an important relationship?

- Do you avoid certain friends or family while you use or drink?

- Do you ever hang out with certain people who you would probably not be with if you weren't using drugs or alcohol?

- While you use or drink, do you ever do things you think are shameful?

- After you use or drink, have you found out that you did things you think are shameful?

Again, there is no magic number of "yes" answers proving you have chemical dependency. However, each "yes" shows you suffer from problems because of using drugs or alcohol. These problems happen because you cannot always predict what will happen when you use or drink. Recognizing these consequences can help you realize you have the symptom of unmanageability as a result of your drug or alcohol use. Unmanageability is a symptom of chemical dependency.

# Chemical Dependency Is Permanent

Remember, having chemical dependency means that you'll often lose your sound judgment (your power and management) when you use drugs or drink alcohol. Sometimes you can avoid consequences while you use or drink, but it's only a temporary interruption to the permanent condition of your dependency. And whenever you do choose to use or drink, you will not always be able to tell how much you will use or drink, or what will happen as a result.

The word *were* in the first step is an important word, representing an important concept for this goal. The concept cannot be defined as literally as *powerless* or *unmanageable*. It means something less identifiable, and yet something crucial to your self-diagnosis and your future plans for recovery.

Bill Wilson was one of the two founders of AA, and the author of *Alcoholics Anonymous*, the guidebook for members of AA. Bill wrote much of the book, including the Twelve Steps, in the past tense. He wanted the reader to understand that, at the time he wrote the book, all the members of AA had already completed the Twelve Steps and had found lasting sobriety. The reader was to learn from the past experiences of the AA membership and then apply what was learned to the reader's own life and recovery.

The first step says that the successfully recovering members of Alcoholics Anonymous had admitted that they "were" powerless and unmanageable. The step doesn't set any time limits on the condition. That is, Bill did *not* write the steps so that this first one could be interpreted to mean "We admitted we were having troubles with drink for the time being, but we could eventually overcome them with a little work and then start drinking again before too long." Bill wrote the steps with the understanding that alcoholism was **permanent**.

That is the concept behind the word *were*. Don't try to take the word too literally. It's the concept that's important, not the word itself: **Chemical dependency is a permanent condition.** All people who have achieved lasting recovery have had to first admit that they *were* chemically dependent people. Once they did that, they could begin the process of recovery.

If you have a chemical dependency, then the symptoms of powerlessness and unmanageability that you identified have lasted for a long time—months, probably years. They aren't merely a series of simple problems that will go away after you decide to stop. These symptoms will occur if you continue to use drugs or alcohol in your future. Your symptoms will not go away just as soon as you get the right job, relationship, or amount money.

# Thinking About the Time Frame of Your Drug or Alcohol Use

Chemical dependency doesn't suddenly invade your life over a few days or weeks. As you think about your signs and symptoms of powerlessness and unmanageability, look for a pattern showing symptoms of permanence. First, think back over the past six months, and then remember even further back. Look hard and look honestly. Recall even the first time you started to drink or use. For example, a patient of mine, John, was forty-three years old. In his thirties, after a decade of moderate drinking, John began to imbibe more and more. He wouldn't have called his drinking heavy. However, in the last six years, John had developed high blood pressure, had been arrested for drunk driving twice, was arguing more frequently with his wife, and his kids were leaving pamphlets on John's favorite chair with titles like *Is AA For You?* His doctor said he was drinking too much. The judge told him he was drinking too much. His wife complained he was drinking too much. His kids were hinting at it. Even though John wouldn't have thought of saying he had alcohol dependency, he had to admit that his biggest problems were being caused by his drinking. It looked to John like there was a pattern, and after six years, he couldn't call it temporary.

Another patient, Brenda, had a less obvious situation. She was twenty-seven, and the mother of three children under the age of six. She had never tried drugs before age twenty-six. A very good mother, she had grown exhausted caring for the kids, keeping house, and working at her job. A friend had offered her speed for several months before she finally agreed to try it after one particularly hard day. She got a lot of work done, but felt ashamed over having done such a thing. Still, a month later she used the drug again. Two months later she was using at least once a week. She prided herself on continuing to be a great mother, though she felt guilty about the drug use. Her friend began charging her for the drug when Brenda began using two hits per week. Her appearance became just a little more sloppy than normal. She lost weight she wasn't trying to lose. She stayed awake more often, but she spent less time in the same room with the kids. Still, no one in Brenda's life noticed anything that looked like trouble, and Brenda wouldn't have volunteered to talk about her drug use.

Brenda realized her trouble after another seven months of using. One of her sons spilled a glass of juice in the box where Brenda hid her supply, ruining two-weeks' worth of drugs. Brenda screamed at him until her son cried and looked at her in terror. Brenda realized she wasn't yelling because of the spilt juice; she was placing her drug use above the security of her child. She also knew that, even though she had used the drug for barely a year, she wasn't going to be able to stop without some heavy-duty help.

If you really haven't had drug- or alcohol-related problems for at least six months, then you probably don't have chemical dependency. You're not off the hook though! You may still need some kind of professional intervention like therapy or drug abuse education, even though you may not need chemical dependency treatment.

Sascha was a college sophomore who had pledged a prestigious sorority. There were many opportunities for her to meet people, get involved, and party. She sampled her first alcohol, ever, at one of the parties. Every weekend the sorority got together with a fraternity for keg parties. She became used to the taste of "Fuzzy Navels,"and the use of "Beer Bongs," but she never got used to the effects of drinking the significant amounts of alcohol she drank. After two months of this, including rush week, Sascha was failing half her classes and had suffered several blackouts while she was drinking. After waking up one morning with a nasty cut on her leg she didn't remember receiving, she came to see me for an evaluation. While she clearly had been abusing alcohol, her situation didn't represent a permanent condition. She needed counseling to cool her socializing and learn to manage her study time better, but she didn't need chemical dependency treatment. Problems with drugs or alcohol that have gone on for less than several months may not indicate chemical dependency. However, if you've had problems with drugs or alcohol that were really bad and frequent in only this short time period, you can still be chemically dependent.

Proof of a pattern doesn't necessarily have to be something that has lasted for any specific length of time. I once assessed a man who tried cocaine for the first time in his fifty-eight years just four months prior to our appointment. He found the effect of the drug fantastic, and the craving to use again irresistible. In four months he had spent his savings account of $60,000 and run up another $30,000 in credit card cash-debits. He wound up in the emergency room with chest pains and received a referral to my office. He had decided even before coming in that he had an addiction. His symptoms weren't long lasting, but they were devastating and couldn't be called the effects of mere temporary abuse.

Has your drug or alcohol use created dramatic problems for you in a fairly short period of time? Well then, keep reading this book. There's an awfully good chance you've got an addiction.

A final tip—be careful when you think about the things you have done in the past. Having just one symptom once a year for ten years doesn't indicate chemical dependency. It probably means you have had other issues going on in your life, maybe emotional issues that only became blatant at those certain times. In that case, see a professional to help you work them out.

# Making an Honest Self-Diagnosis

While reading this, you've probably talked yourself into and out of a self-diagnosis of being chemically dependent several times. It's time to make a formal self-diagnosis. You need to create two lists of symptoms proving to yourself that you are chemically dependent. Soon to come in this section you'll record these symptoms on two worksheets. Then you will make an actual diagnosis for yourself based on the symptoms you name. However, there are a few things you should consider first.

As you do this work, you'll probably feel yourself resist taking an honest look at your situation. While this is natural—even expected—it won't help you. It can be hard to make an honest self-diagnosis because you know what comes next: If you know you have a chemical dependency, then you know you should treat it.

## *Facing Denial*

Denial comes in different forms. The most obvious form of denial is to simply claim that something isn't so. When you think over your years of drug or alcohol misuse, you keep saying, "There were never any problems." Or, despite some incredible evidence, symptoms, and proof that you're aware of, you insist you do not have a drug or alcohol problem. I have visited patients in the hospital with liver damage, jaundiced skin, and intestinal bleeding who insisted their problem wasn't caused by alcohol, but by eating spicy foods. I have also talked with prisoners in jail for repeated drug offenses who insist the only reason they're incarcerated is because the police don't like their families.

Denial isn't always so obvious, however. Another way that resistance and denial can show up is if you try to downplay how severe some of your symptoms have been. You might overlook how dangerous, tragic, or serious some of those problems have been. Or you might insist that the problems wouldn't have been that bad except that someone else made them worse. "If it weren't for that other big-mouth," you might claim, "the situation never would have turned into a catastrophe."

You might want to insist that your symptoms happened only because of something else, not because of your use of drugs or alcohol. In these cases, for example, you might say it wasn't fair that you got arrested—the police actually trapped you. Or, you might say the reason you had negative job consequences was because you boss doesn't like you. You tell yourself that your frequent use of drugs or alcohol didn't really matter in the situation.

A crafty form of denial is found in a patient I worked with only one time. Stan, a thirty-eight-year-old father, came on referral from another therapist who works in the same clinic as I. He began the session describing the trouble his fifteen-year-old son was causing to the family. When I asked him to discuss his drinking or drug use, he exploded in a tirade.

Stan said that three therapists had already told him that his son's behavior would not improve until he did something about his drinking and use of marijuana. His voice raised to a shout as he declared that his drinking was his business, and that he was responsible enough to use marijuana on occasion. He pointed out that his son also drank and used marijuana, but that he was immature and incapable of making responsible decisions. Stan ridiculed me and my profession. He said he had the finances and the savvy to take care of the trouble his alcohol use had caused. He said none of the professionals he'd seen looked at the real trouble in the family, which was his son. He wrapped up his harangue saying he wouldn't let his life or his family be pushed around by the incorrigible behavior of a sophomore in high school, and that all the counselors he'd seen as well as his wife refused to understand this.

I began to explain that his son might be reacting to the trouble Stan said his drinking had caused. Stan then got up, swore at me, and left my office. On the way out, he filed a complaint to my supervisor stating I refused to help his family. He never did do anything about his drinking or drug use; his denial got in the way of his taking an honest look at his family's real problem.

Resistance is more subtle than denial. Resistance is a tactic that postpones an honest evaluation of signs and symptoms. I usually see resistance in the form of a potential patient making appointments but then never showing; or agreeing to pursue treatment, but insisting it can't happen until later on. If you got this book several months ago, and are only now taking a look at it, you've been resistant!

Resistance can also come in the form of vague answers. When I've asked patients to tell me about their drinking, I'll often get an answer like, "Oh, gee, I don't drink that much that often." Sometimes a patient will say they can't remember the details of their drug- or alcohol-related problems. They say they can't remember if they've ever been arrested, how much money they've spent, how long they've used drugs or alcohol, or whether or not their significant others have ever complained about their use. That's not answering a question, that's resistance. Remember this as you think about your own situation and write down your own answers. Honesty is not vague.

Denial is also often the reason you may choose to not mention some of the important things that have happened because of your drug or alcohol use. Perhaps some of your consequences and symptoms are too embarrassing for you to really face. Maybe you don't want anyone else to know about them. So, you might feel inclined to not include those consequences when you make your lists of symptoms. Unfortunately, denial of truth doesn't change the truth; it only perpetuates your problems. Denial will only weaken your self-diagnosis. If you cannot be honest with yourself, then you will not make an honest self-diagnosis. If you don't have an honest self-diagnosis, then whatever you do to treat yourself will not be a strong and honest effort. It might work for a while, but not in the long run.

One way you can help yourself overcome denial and resistance is to work on this goal with someone you can trust. You might consider the help of a therapist or counselor who knows about chemical dependency, or maybe enlist the help of a trusted friend or family member. Whoever you choose, make sure he or she is someone you can trust and who's feedback you can accept. At the very least, it's a good idea to check your recovery work on this goal with another person when you think you have finished. It would even be better if you could find that person before you finish your work so that you can stop yourself from holding back on your self-diagnosis through resistance and denial.

There are other ways you can mess up your chances for a good self-diagnosis. Denial and resistance take many forms. Think about the following suggestions as you do your work:

*Avoid comparing your use of drugs and alcohol with that of anyone else.* You can probably name several people who use or drink more than you do. You might even know a few who *always* use more than you do, and who use or drink more often than you. Does that mean, you might wonder, that your problem isn't as bad as their problem, and that therefore you don't really have chemical dependency? **No.**

Trying to excuse yourself by comparing yourself against the behavior of others weakens your self-diagnosis. If you do this, you probably do it in order to keep from taking an honest look at your own problem. That kind of game-playing will sidetrack your self-diagnosis. Only think about your own behavior. Think about what happens to you when you drink or use drugs.

*Avoid using other people's "hassles" about your drug use or drinking as an excuse to use.* You've probably argued with others about your drinking or drug use. Maybe you even resent their criticisms, their frequent judgments, and their suspicions about you. It's probably easy to justify your drinking or drug use as a way to get even with them, as a way to make them angry, or as a way to show them that you're the boss of your life, not them.

You won't get very far in a self-diagnosis if you continue to let yourself do this. Remember, if you have a lot of the symptoms of chemical dependency, then other people have noticed them too. For this process, don't worry about their anger, suspicions, and re-actions; just look at yourself and your own drug and alcohol use.

*Avoid trying to claim that since you never try to limit your drug or alcohol use, you cannot really say whether or not you really do lose control.* Some chemically dependent people never try to limit their use, others never have any fixed amount in mind when they start. These people just drink or use until they stop. You might try to say that you just use or drink until it's gone, and that's all there is to it. Therefore, you never really do lose your ability to predict how much of the drug or alcohol you will use.

This is an example of looking at one kind of a symptom only. If you never plan to limit your drinking or drug use, then that is a sign that your use may be out of control. If your drug or alcohol is so important that you make sure you never run out, that indicates you've lost the ability to regulate your consumption. You proba-bly don't keep an unlimited supply of green beans around you, right? You'd be okay if you ran out of beans; what is it about drugs or alcohol that make them so important to you? Sounds like you're dealing with an example of the concept of powerlessness.

While you work on the following assignments, try to avoid denial and resistance. Work on these assignments with someone else, if necessary. Avoid rationalizing your use of drugs or alcohol; it will hurt your chances for a good job on your self-diagnosis. If you can avoid those pitfalls to honesty, you will make a good self-diagnosis. Okay, now you're ready to do the work.

# Writing Down Your Signs and Symptoms

First, think of the symptoms showing your drug or alcohol may be unmanageable. Most people find these examples easier to come up with than examples of powerlessness. As mentioned, these symptoms are easier to notice.

Remember, these ten examples should show that you cannot always tell what will happen when you choose to use drugs or alcohol. Again, think about the problems you have had because of your drug or alcohol use—problems that you wouldn't have had if you hadn't used or drank. Think about the consequences your drug or alcohol use has caused you with your family, friends, work, the law, your finances, health, or with your reputation.

Ten examples is a minimum. The more you can think of, the more certain you can make your self-diagnosis. You can write more examples in your journal.

### Unmanageability

Here are ten examples showing I cannot always *manage or handle* things when I choose to use drugs or drink:

1. _____

   _____

2. _____

   _____

3. _____

   _____

4. _____

5. _____

6. _____

7. _____

8. _____

9. _____

10. _____

Next, write down examples showing you have symptoms of powerlessness when you use drugs or drink. This time, think about the questions you answered on the pages discussing powerlessness. Again, write down at least ten examples.

## Powerlessness

Here are ten examples showing that I cannot always tell *how much* I will use or drink when I choose to use drugs or drink alcohol:

1. _____

2. _____

3. _____

4. _____

_____

5. _____

_____

6. _____

_____

7. _____

_____

8. _____

_____

9. _____

_____

10. _____

_____

Take a moment to study the two lists you've just finished. What do they mean to you? Do you suffer from a pattern of powerlessness and unmanageability when you choose to drink alcohol or use drugs? Do your lists prove to you that you have chemical dependency? Answer this question on a third piece of paper, or a third page from your journal. You don't *have* to show anyone this answer, so be honest. Make a self-diagnosis.

Autumn, a patient in her thirties, gives a good example of how this part of the process works. Autumn and I had discussed her drinking and drug use over the course of three sessions. She acknowledged that, over ten years' time, her drinking had gone from appropriate socializing to unpredictable jags. She was drinking a bottle of wine at least four times a week. In the first session she tried to insist that wine really wasn't alcohol, like liquor. She also maintained that, since she had never been arrested, she couldn't really have an alcohol problem. Over the sessions, however, as she completed her lists of examples of powerlessness and unmanageability, she came to realize that many problems in her life were caused by her drinking.

She had never been arrested because she got rides or traveled everywhere by taxi when she was drinking. In the last six years, she had spent enough money on cab fare to have purchased a car. She called that a "waste of money" and a symptom of unmanageability. Other symptoms included the fact that she had been reprimanded at work for abusing sick leave to nurse her hangovers. She had destroyed two important relationships, including one engagement, because of her drinking. She had noticed that her good friends were avoiding her, and that she had only seen them in the last year at events where alcohol would not be served. As for powerlessness, she reported that if she opened a bottle of wine, she was going to drink the whole bottle—no exceptions. This is the way things had been for at least five years, and she believed things would continue like this if she kept drinking.

In the past six months, she convinced her physician to prescribe tranquilizers to help her calm down. Almost immediately, she found that she could drink alcohol on top of the drug, and increase the effects of both. Twice, she renewed prescriptions for the drug early by telling her physician her purse had been stolen and the drugs with it. She considered lying to her doctor another sign of unmanageability.

Autumn wanted to blame her friends, her boyfriends, and her physician for causing all her stress. With a little prodding, however, she gave up that resistance and focused on her real problem. Autumn had a drinking problem, and the tranquilizers had become a problem too. She couldn't think of a way or a time that she could drink or use the drugs without winding up drunk or strung out. She admitted that she had chemical dependency, putting it this way: "I believe I am an addict because I believe I have lost the ability to control my drinking or use of tranquilizers *forever*." She didn't rejoice in her newfound understanding, but she said it was a relief to admit it.

Think about all the symptoms you came up with. Do these symptoms show only a surprising, short-term run of bad luck? That is, are your symptoms something that will go away by themselves if you wait long enough? Or do your symptoms show something more? Do they show that you have a long-term problem? Have these symptoms gone on long enough for you, or anyone, to say they are a permanent pattern? Are you convinced that these symptoms aren't going to go away by themselves?

To finish this goal, write down your self-diagnosis in a way that you can understand. See if you can't make it something other people *could* understand, too.

### Self-Diagnosis

Finish this sentence in detail, perhaps including some of your symptoms. **After studying my signs and symptoms, my self-diagnosis is:**

_____

_____

_____

_____

_____

# What to Do with Your Self-Diagnosis

After all that work, you should now have a finished product: A self-diagnosis. Your self-diagnosis looks like one of the following three options: either you know you have chemical dependency; or you've discovered that you've got a problem but not dependency; or you know you have dependency but don't care enough right now to proceed with a recovery process. Each one of these diagnoses now requires you to move on in one way or another.

*Did you make a self-diagnosis that shows you have chemical dependency?* If you have proven to yourself that you have powerlessness and unmanageability because of your drug or alcohol use and this is a permanent problem, then you have diagnosed yourself as chemically dependent. Congratulations.

Diagnosing yourself as having chemical dependency is a serious issue. Doing so shows humility and maturity. If you can face the truth of your situation, then you have what it takes to overcome it. Time to move on. The next chapter will help you get started with your recovery.

*Did your self-diagnosis show you* do not *have chemical dependency?* If, however, you absolutely, honestly couldn't come up with twenty examples of symptoms of the permanent problem of chemical dependency—no matter how long and how hard you tried to think of them—then you may not have chemical dependency. In that case, you could not have diagnosed yourself with chemical dependency. The diagnosis wouldn't have been accurate if you didn't have the symptoms.

If you don't have chemical dependency, but you still have a drug or alcohol problem, then you have some other kind of problem that you should address. You should find some counselor or helper who could help you get more insight into your situation. Do this so you can keep the problem from getting worse, possibly even going on to become chemical dependency. Even if you do not have chemical dependency, you might still find the guidelines for change in this book helpful. Try reading on to see if this book can help you make changes to reduce the problems you have because of drugs or alcohol. Maybe you can still benefit from considering alternatives to drinking and drug use. Clearly, your drug or alcohol use is not helping your life. A change might not be a bad idea for you.

In any event, this book is geared toward you assuming that you have diagnosed yourself with chemical dependency. The rest of the book will help you learn how to recover.

*Do you have all the symptoms but don't want to admit you have chemical dependency?* On the other hand, if your examples show you have enough of the symptoms but you still refuse to diagnose yourself as having chemical dependency, then you have too much resistance to let this process work. If this is the case, treatment and recovery will not work for you right now. You're denying the diagnosis that the symptoms suggest. Perhaps you should reexamine your symptoms of powerlessness and unmanageability and see if you change your mind.

The permanent nature of chemical dependency means the symptoms will happen again in your future. If you want to avoid such problems in your future, then you need to commit to making changes. That cannot begin without a self-diagnosis. If you just won't make a diagnosis, you should discuss this with a professional chemical dependency counselor or therapist. No process will work for you right now. You need a change in your outlook. Work on making that change with someone else, and then return to this book when you are ready to diagnose yourself with chemical dependency.

## Reaching Your First Goal

Chemical dependency is a problem whereby when you choose to use drugs or alcohol, you cannot always predict how much you will drink or use, and you cannot always predict the consequences of your drinking or using. When you have chemical dependency, you do not exercise sound judgment—at least when you drink or use. As a result, your whole lifestyle suffers in some way or another. If you've been able to make a self-diagnosis saying that you have the problem, then you can begin to treat it. Making a self-diagnosis that you can understand puts you in charge of your treatment from the very beginning. You've accomplished your first goal!

Each one of these goals has a therapeutic goal statement that goes with it. When you finish the work on each goal, you will be able to make the statements your own. The statement for the first goal explains all the work you've done in one sentence:

> *I admit I am unable to always tell how much I will use or drink when I choose to use drugs or alcohol, nor can I always tell what will happen when I choose to use or drink.*

After you have diagnosed yourself with chemical dependency, your recovery can begin. Chapter 2 will help you identify what you will need to help you with your recovery.

# 2

# Identify Your Sources of Support

Now you know you have a chemical dependency. Your second goal, which will help you start the recovery process, is to begin naming people and things that can help you change your lifestyle into one that helps you keep sound judgment. In other words, who and what are your sources of support? This goal uses concepts from the second step in the Twelve Steps. The second step reads: "Came to believe that a Power greater than ourselves could restore us to sanity." That sentence calls for some important action. The recovery process in this book also requires important action on your part.

However, in this process, the focus of your recovery doesn't have to be spiritual as in the focus of the Twelve Steps. In this chapter, you will identify the sources of support in your life that may or may not be spiritually based. There are two important concepts from step two that help make this goal. The concepts behind both these terms are important and need a lot of explanation. Understanding the concept of *sanity* will help you get a better grasp of what your recovery must include. Understanding the concept behind "Power greater than ourselves" will help you clarify who and what in your life can help you get it.

### "Sanity"

In the 1930s, *sanity* was understood as meaning "the state of being sane, or having soundness of judgment." The word *sane* was understood to mean "of sound mind . . . having or exercising reason, sound judgment, or good sense." As you see, sanity didn't necessarily refer to mental health or mental illness. In other words, you don't have to be crazy to have chemical dependency. Instead, this concept means that you have lost your ability to maintain sound judgment because of your chemical dependency. Your recovery has to be based upon restoring your sound judgment.

In this recovery process, restoring your sanity involves getting back what you admitted you had lost in your first goal: *your sound judgment.* When you use or drink, remember, you lose your power and your manageability over drugs and alcohol. When you lose that power and management, you cannot exercise sound judgment.

How can you get back your sound judgment? Well, if you choose to avoid drinking alcohol and using drugs, you'll never again lose your sound judgment; at least, not because of drugs or alcohol. An easy thing to say, but a hard commitment to make. You will need your sources of support to help you follow through with this commitment.

# Abstinence—A Must for Recovery

If you have chemical dependency, you cannot learn how to drink or use again on a social basis and still exercise sound judgment. If you start to drink or use again, you'll have problems again. This is true even if you go for a long time without alcohol or drugs, and then start up again. Remember what you learned in chapter 1: Chemical dependency is a permanent problem, not just an unfortunate and temporary run of bad luck. Therefore, you can recover only if you never use drugs or alcohol. This is called *abstinence.*

When you stay away from using drugs and alcohol, you "abstain" from drugs and alcohol.

If you have chemical dependency, you'll be able to restore sound judgment in your life if you abstain from drugs or alcohol. This is the only way. And you know what? Your abstinence has to begin with this goal—this is how you'll begin to restore sound judgment to your life.

## There's No Denying the Need for Abstinence

Abstinence is a hard commitment to make. In the last twenty-five years, researchers and therapists have tried to figure out ways to let people keep drinking or using drugs as part of the treatment for chemical dependency. Their research has been unsuccessful. Of course, some people with drinking problems—but not a real alcohol *dependency*—have learned how to drink without problems. People who can do this are people who've never had permanent patterns of problems with their drinking.

However, there is absolutely no proven effective way for alcohol dependent people to become "social drinkers." Furthermore, no one can help people addicted to illicit drugs to learn how to become "social drug users." Do you think abstinence is too much to ask you to do? If you still want to defend your right to drink or use drugs, then you should return to chapter 1 and study all the work you did to finish that goal.

Consider, again, your use of drugs or alcohol. As you think about your history with drugs or alcohol, think about the consequences your drinking or drug use caused you. Remember that you named those consequences a sign of a *permanent problem*. Do you still think you can manage some "social" drug or alcohol use in light of your history? Your drug or alcohol use has gotten you into so much trouble already that you have sought ways to treat yourself. At the very least, you have sought the advice in this book. If you have looked for that kind of help, then you should understand you cannot drink or use in a *social* way ever. If you could have done it, you already would have.

Now, you've probably maintained some periods of abstinence in your past, right? However, your problems and consequences most likely appeared shortly after you began to drink or use again. This doesn't happen to people who can manage "social" use of drugs or alcohol. If you could have stayed a "social" user or drinker, you would still be one. Your chemical dependency is a permanent condition that will go into *remission* (that means, disappear) when you make a committed effort to abstain. If you begin using drugs or alcohol again, you'll eventually lose your sound judgment soon thereafter. Eventually, your problems will reemerge. When this happens, there goes your remission. When you start to use drugs or drink again, it's called *relapse.*

Relapse might seem surprising and unexpected to you at the point when you realize you are relapsing or have just done it. However, you relapse only because you give up your commitment to abstinence and begin using or drinking again. Your recovery must include abstinence. If you don't abstain from drugs and alcohol, you'll not recover.

## Withdrawal Symptoms

There's something else that can make abstinence seem difficult, especially as you just get started—withdrawal. You will find the early part of your recovery difficult if you suffer withdrawal symptoms. Withdrawal symptoms don't always occur. However, when they do, they make you feel uncomfortable. Withdrawal symptoms are the reaction your mind and body might have when you stop using drugs or alcohol. Most withdrawal is slight, some is severe. With drug dependencies, for example, physical withdrawal symptoms can range from moderately irritating to downright dangerous. Withdrawing from just about any drug—alcohol, marijuana, uppers or downers—can make you feel irritable, edgy, quick-tempered, and depressed. Those symptoms may last a few days to a few months, and can range from hardly noticeable to severe.

If you withdraw from stimulants like cocaine, crystal methamphetamine, or uppers like "ice" or "batu," you may also experience nervousness, anxiety, and restlessness. You might suffer from sleep problems like insomnia, sleeping too much, not being able to stay asleep, and strange dreams. You could also have mood swings, appetite changes, and unexpected cravings for stimulants (especially sugar, caffeine, and nicotine). Some people suffer from itchiness and muscle twitches.

Depressants are drugs like barbiturates "downers," tranquilizers, opiates like heroin and pain pills, alcohol, marijuana, and sleep aids. These kinds of drugs can produce the same kinds of withdrawal symptoms as the stimulants. In addition, you could also experience some body aches and bowel problems like constipation or diarrhea.

Here's an odd fact about marijuana, cocaine, and crystal methamphetamine. When you withdraw from these drugs, you might have dreams in which you use them. Some of my patients have been very disturbed by how realistic those "using dreams" can seem. You might wake up feeling guilty, not quite sure if your drug use was really a dream or not.

Withdrawal symptoms, if they occur, start off strong, then quickly reduce in intensity. The first few days of abstinence are always the worst for any drug withdrawal. After two to four weeks, withdrawal symptoms are almost always mild. Usually, by that time, withdrawal symptoms include just sleep troubles, some cravings, and mood swings. Although withdrawal symptoms do taper off, they can in their milder forms last for several months.

With alcohol and with benzodiazepines like Xanax or Valium, however, the trauma on your body could be deadly for the first few days after you begin to abstain. If you're recovering from alcohol or benzodiazepines, you should definitely seek some help when you begin your recovery. A physician who has had training in the field of chemical dependency should help you through any potentially dangerous withdrawal. When you seek this sort of help you must report your drug and alcohol use with blunt honesty. Tell the doctor what you used, how much, how often, and for how long. Only then will the doctor know the best care to prescribe for your withdrawal, if indeed you need such help. Fortunately, in most cases your life will not be in danger from withdrawal symptoms. A doctor will most likely advise you to get plenty of sleep, eat an excellent diet, and find sober and drug-free people to support you.

# Tips on Handling Withdrawal

Not everyone experiences particularly noticeable withdrawal symptoms. If you do, however, or if you know you will because you have before, then there are some things you can do to lessen their severity and how they affect you. Read this section, then think of what you can do right now, in the next few days, and over the next three months to help you deal with the discomfort of no longer using drugs or alcohol. Remember, these are guidelines only. You should seek professional advice for specific details or to determine whether or not your health could suffer as you follow these guidelines.

## Eat Well

As your body recovers from your use of drugs or alcohol, it needs energy and protein to help repair itself. Your body gets that energy and protein from what you eat and drink. However, you shouldn't eat or drink things your body can use as a substitute for drugs or alcohol. Therefore, you should avoid junk food, sugary food, fatty food, or drinks containing caffeine.

Right now, your wisest choices for food are *complex carbohydrates* and *high-protein* foods. For complex carbohydrates, you should eat a lot of fresh or steamed vegetables and fruits, pasta, beans, and rice. Good sources of protein include lean meats, beans, chicken, fish, tofu, and low-fat milk products. These foods will give your body the energy and building blocks it needs to repair itself and help you become healthier. Avoid anything that comes out of a can or almost anything served by fast-food restaurants.

There's a good chance your body might not know what to do with all that healthy stuff. You might experience some gas or diarrhea for a while. That will subside as your body gets used to digesting real food again, and stops relying on drugs or alcohol to provide it with all the energy it used to get.

## Sleep Well

Another important thing for you to do is to get plenty of sleep. How much? That varies from person to person. In general, get as much as you need to feel refreshed all the next day. That might mean going to bed earlier than you're used to, or even letting yourself sleep in. The important thing is to get yourself on a schedule so you get plenty of sleep to give your body more opportunity to repair and refresh itself.

If you suffer from insomnia, or if you can't stay asleep once you fall asleep, you should do some techniques to help your body get used to your new schedule. If you can't fall asleep after twenty minutes, then get out of bed. Then do anything you want, as long as it's not watching television. Read, for example, or clean house, do the dishes, iron clothes, write letters, or write in your journal. This occupies your time so you don't become too frustrated. Being out of bed helps you learn not to dread your bed as a source of conflict. Leaving the TV off keeps you from getting worked up over whatever might be on the tube, like an action show or an erotic show. Eventually, while doing these things, you're going to become tired. Go to bed and give yourself another twenty minutes. If you're still not asleep, then do it all over again. It may seem frustrating over the course of several nights, but you'll get onto a schedule eventually. Make sure that when it's time to get out of bed, you do it. Don't linger. That will also help you develop good sleep habits. Pretty soon you'll probably fall asleep and stay asleep without any problem. If you don't, then it might be time to see a doctor.

## Get Adequate Exercise

Aerobic exercise, the kind that makes you breathe hard, helps your body heal. It helps you build stamina, and in the long run it helps you relax, get better sleep, and maybe need less sleep. Exercise also helps your body get rid of the residual drug still in your body for the first few days or even weeks.

The amount of exercise necessary to help you is less daunting than you might imagine. All it takes is something three times a week for twenty to thirty minutes that makes you breathe harder than normal, and gets your heart beating faster than normal. There are benefits to modest exercise—the kind that revs you up, but doesn't make you sweat too much. Still, the benefits to hard exercise are even better for your body's health and healing, even at just three times a week for a half hour. Try taking the time to walk briskly for twenty minutes three times each week and see if you don't feel a little better at the end of a month.

## Find Healthy Companionship

One of the worst parts of suffering withdrawal is the feeling of isolation and loneliness you may endure. You might think there's no one who can understand how you feel or what you're going through. Well, there are other people who have experienced similar kinds of withdrawal as yours. There are also people who may not have suffered the kinds of withdrawal you have, but who can still understand what you must be going through. You should find those people, get to know them a little, let them know you a little, and talk about your withdrawal and your recovery.

Later in this chapter, you will learn more about the importance of attending support groups and finding individuals who can help you in your recovery. For now, know that your chances for lasting recovery are better if you include people who can support you in your recovery process. These kinds of people such as sympathetic friends, members of recovery-oriented support groups, or qualified professionals can reassure you that the way you feel is normal. You can also rely on their word that any withdrawal you experience will eventually end. They can be a shoulder for you to lean upon. They can give you advice, comfort, and support.

You don't have to endure withdrawal symptoms all by yourself. In fact, you shouldn't. Find some compassionate support to help you through. Once your withdrawal symptoms have diminished, these people will probably be able to help you in other aspects of your recovery.

## Plan a Strategy

If you experience noticeable withdrawal symptoms that get in the way of your daily routine, the best way to deal with them is to come up with a plan of action and stick to it. If you could develop this plan before you stop using or drinking, that would be even better. However, don't read that last sentence as permission to go out and use or drink one more time so you can withdrawal the right way!

Try this: Think of how you'd handle these four situations; write down your answers on a piece of paper if you want. Either way, you'll be making a plan of action to help you deal with relapse. Write down some specific plans for the following:

- How could you eat healthier while you withdraw? Make a menu, or make a list of the things you will eat every day. You might also consider writing down the things you won't eat or drink. Example: I'll stick to salad, fish, chicken, and raw fruit. I'll avoid my usual snacks, ice cream, and sodas.

- How could you sleep better while you withdraw? Again, write down a plan. What could you do to get a better night's sleep? What could you do to not get as frustrated if you can't fall asleep. How's this: If I can't fall asleep within twenty minutes, I'll get out of bed and read a novel in my chair until I feel tired. I won't drink any caffeine after 3 PM, because caffeine will keep me awake if I drink it later. I'll go to bed every night by 11 PM, and get out of bed for the day by 7 AM.

- How could you get decent exercise while you withdraw? Exercise is important, and you don't even have to create a Herculean regimen for yourself. Just make sure you get out of the house at least three times each week and move yourself quickly. Here's a plan: I'll walk to and from work every day, and walk at a brisk pace when I return home. Or: Instead of watching the morning news, I'll walk for twenty minutes.

- How can you get healthy companionship? Find some support for yourself and your recovery. You'll feel better knowing that someone understands how you feel. Who can you talk to? Where will you find them? What will you say? See if your plan can't look something like this: I will tell my spouse, my best friend, that I'm coming off my drug, and that I'm going to feel lousy for a while. I'll go to that support group I heard about last year, and see what they have to say about withdrawal symptoms. I'll make it a point to call my friend every day at 8 PM to check in and to say that I'm okay.

Finally, don't forget to give yourself reassurance. Remind yourself every day that withdrawal symptoms, while uncomfortable, are a sign that your body is getting better, your mind can get better, and that you've spent another day free from alcohol or drugs. Use your support, diet, exercise, and sleep plans to reassure yourself that you're getting better, despite how miserable you might feel. Withdrawal symptoms are *always temporary*. Give yourself a week, and you'll be feeling better. Another week and you'll be feeling much better. A month and you'll just be that much more relieved.

Now, back to work on restoring your sound judgment.

# Do You Have to Abstain from Both Drugs and Alcohol?

Yes. Abstinence means you must stay away from both alcohol and drugs, even drugs that you don't normally use. There are a few reasons for this.

First of all, many drugs affect your body in similar ways. You could actually trade addictions by using one drug that was similar to your "drug of choice." Using that kind of drug teases your body into wanting more. If you have alcohol dependency, for example, you would be a high risk for relapse if you ever used drugs which affect your body similarly to alcohol, like Valium or Xanax. If you preferred an upper, like cocaine, it would be unwise if you chose to use another upper, like crystal methamphetamine.

Sometimes, your body can begin to crave a very different drug. This will happen if you use an abuseable drug while you try to stop using another one. For example, as you try to give up co- caine, you might find that you start to enjoy alcohol—especially because alcohol takes the edge off cocaine withdrawal. Before too long, you would develop a problem with alcohol.

Likewise, if you're trying to stop using alcohol or marijuana, you shouldn't use stimulants like cocaine or amphetamines. You could easily transfer your addiction to them. Your recovery requires abstinence. You need to abstain from both alcohol and drugs.

## The Exception to this Rule—Cigarettes

If you already smoke cigarettes, it would be the wisest choice to stop smoking now. However, over the years, the field of recov- ery has given smokers a break. People have been able to recover from chemical dependency while continuing to smoke cigarettes.

If you already smoke, and you can't tolerate the withdrawal symptoms when you try to stop, then you don't have to stop *right now*. Perhaps you could in a while, after you have maintained your abstinence and recovery. Just don't increase the number of cigarettes you smoke in a day. If you do, you'll only tease your body into wanting even more. Then you'll want something stronger. Then you run the risk of relapse. If you don't smoke now, don't start! There's absolutely no way that would help your recovery.

Incidentally, the same is true if you use caffeine. Caffeine is a stimulant. It can tease your body as much as cocaine or amphetamines. Your healthiest choice is to not drink coffee, black tea, or caffeinated sodas and colas. If you do drink these kinds of beverages, then keep your use to a minimum. No more than two modest servings per day would be the best idea. It's important to your recovery.

## Do You Automatically Relapse if You Fail in Your Abstinence?

All this talk about abstinence might make you think that you'll fail in your recovery for good if you so much as smell liquor. Well, truth is, that's not exactly the case. If you maintain abstinence for a while—say, at least a year or more—and then use or drink on an occasion again, by accident or on purpose, it is possible that the end result might be nothing at all; that you don't dive back into your drug or alcohol use full-fledged. It's a risky thing, however, and nothing that you want to test yourself on. There is no guarantee that you won't relapse in those situations.

### By Accident

In some cases, as a recovering chemically dependent person, you may not know about the alcohol content of a particular food, a drink, or some kind of medication. You may not realize that someone has spiked your punch at a party. Or, you might need to take pain medication that a physician prescribed to you after an accident or surgery. A doctor might suggest that you take an over-the-counter medication containing alcohol or stimulants to help relieve the symptoms of a cold or allergies. You might have to have painful dental work and need mood-altering pain medication. Similar situations can occur anytime in your recovery, even after just a few months of abstinence.

If you use drugs or alcohol in this way it doesn't necessarily mean that you have relapsed—that is, returned to your out-of-control use of drugs or alcohol. What it means is that you may need to anticipate and plan for unexpected events that can threaten your lasting abstinence. You'll learn this kind of planning over time—chapters eight and nine will teach you the skills in more detail. For now, just know that you will need some guidance eventually to help you deal with accidental use.

### On Purpose

What if you *decide* to have a drink or use a drug at a family function or at a business meeting? There is a chance, perhaps even a good chance, that you could have a successful try at this kind of "social" use, just like you hoped. If that happens, red flags should go off in your mind. Remember, your recovery began with the first goal when you admitted that you couldn't *always predict what your drug or alcohol use would be like*. Taking this kind of a risk with your abstinence will probably lead you to try "social" use again, and then again, and then again, and then . . .

Given enough trials, you'll find that you can't maintain the abstinence you'd hoped for when you began your recovery. You'd have given up your commitment to abstinence. You'd have returned to your dependency in full swing and relapsed. So, there is no such thing as voluntary use without it being a relapse.

Testing yourself like that has no guarantee of success, even just one time. If you really want to recover, you can't try to learn how to be more clever at avoiding consequences. Recovery isn't learning how to avoid consequences. Recovery means learning how to develop and maintain a healthier lifestyle; a lifestyle free from using drugs or alcohol; a lifestyle based on sound judgment. That means a lifestyle based on abstinence. Now, on to how to start developing that lifestyle.

# A "Power Greater Than Ourselves" is a "Source of Support" for Your Abstinence

A commitment to abstain from drugs and alcohol may seem overwhelming, particularly because you don't know how to do it yet. Well, to learn how, you need to identify what or who can help you maintain your abstinence, thereby recovering your sound judgment. Take a look at the original second step's term "Power greater than ourselves." This term hints of a heavenly force. The capitalized "P" suggests something Godlike. Today, many people don't like these kinds of ideas.

With the process in this book, you don't have to identify an authoritative or heavenly "Power." In this recovery process, identify anything or anyone who can provide you with a healthy, new direction for your life. By identifying these people and things for yourself, *you* keep yourself in charge of your recovery.

To stay abstinent, you need some outside help. Remember, with the first goal you admitted that you had lost your sound judgment because of your drinking or drug use. You can restore the sound judgment you lost with help from sources besides yourself.

This term "power" simply refers to someone or something that possesses or exercises authority or influence. You want to identify something that can influence you. That influence needs to be greater than your own influence—in terms of knowing how to abstain from drugs and alcohol. This guidance and influence could come from a person or a thing.

This goal doesn't require you to find a "Power greater than yourself." However, you do need to find sources of support that can help you get and keep your sound judgment. You're in charge of what sources of support you'll name and use.

Natasha, an addict I was treating, was getting frustrated with her therapy because she wasn't getting any better. I suggested several times that she involve other people in her recovery, but she had resisted this. We worked together for six weeks, and she never managed to go more than five days without using drugs.

After her latest use, we spoke intensely about Natasha's reluctance. It was time for Natasha to make a commitment or to take a leave of absence from therapy for a while. She began to cry as she recounted the number of people who she felt had pushed her around in her life. Her parents, church, boyfriends, and supervisors had often made her feel obligated to do anything they demanded, even if Natasha felt hurt by it. She was afraid that by identifying sources to support her recovery, she would be setting herself up to humiliation, judgment, and ridicule by those people and things.

I assured her that this wasn't the way it was supposed to work. She needed to identify people who she could *trust to help her* without hurting her. We both agreed it might be best for her to identify mostly compassionate women to aid Natasha's recovery.

Natasha did identify several women friends, a support group, and a woman she knew who was a member of a self-help group for sobriety; all of whom Natasha thought could help her. Her sources were strict at times, but never demeaning. They helped her identify even more people and another group that helped her, and Natasha enrolled in a class that gave her even more stamina to avoid drinking and using drugs. With all that help, Natasha was able to do what she had been unable to do on her own. She's still sober after three years.

## Identifying Your Sources of Support

Now you'll figure out what people and things could help you get and stay abstinent. Many different people and things can help you do something you have otherwise been unable to do. Therefore, they become a source of support for you. They can help you stick with your abstinence and your overall recovery from chemical dependency. There are more sources of support for abstinence than any one person could name. Consider all the different kinds of sources of support. These could include the following people:

- Counselor
- Therapist
- Social worker
- Practitioner
- Medical professional
- Health care professional
- Teacher
- Inspirational speaker
- Trustworthy family member
- Friend who respects your need to maintain abstinence
- Others who have personal experience in maintaining abstinence
- Sponsor from a Twelve-Step group
- Other support group members

A source of support doesn't necessarily have to be another person. Consider other sources like:

- Support groups: AA, NA, Women for Sobriety, Secular Organizations for Sobriety, or Rational Recovery

- Civic organizations

- Books such as this one for chemical dependency recovery (Most larger bookstores devote whole sections to recovery literature, and you could easily locate books in a library.)

- Disciplined activities: such as martial arts or yoga

- Activities that help you abstain: organized sports, a hobby, or attending school

- Personal commitment to become a better partner, parent, child, or employee

You can find books or other kinds of literature that aren't specifically recovery books, but that still support your abstinence. Many people find inspiration from autobiographies written by men, women, and children who have overcome obstacles of illness, heartbreak, and trauma. You might get some inspiration from their stories. Of course, people who have overcome chemical dependency have written dozens of books about their recovery also. Larger bookstores set aside entire sections for books on recovery.

Many people have found that an idea, rather than an actual thing, can help them maintain abstinence. Many of my patients have used their desire to be a better parent as one of their sources of support. Others have used their religious beliefs to help motivate and support them. Some other recovering chemically dependent people have found nature to be something permanent, something they believe they can rely upon to *be there*, regardless of whatever happens in their lives. People take comfort in knowing that even if they cannot count on their ability to stay abstinent today, they can count on something like the tides still ebbing and flowing or a big tree standing tall against the sky. If they can rely on nature to always be there for them, that gives them the inspiration to rely on their commitment to stay away from drugs and alcohol permanently, also. Nature gives them an example to follow.

Makana, a thirty-three-year-old patient of mine, is a good example of this. Makana was an independent, but drug-addicted man. He felt awkward around people, and preferred the solitude of using drugs, surfing, and other outdoor activities like gardening to more social pursuits. He was court-ordered into treatment, and was anxious about having to go to Twelve-Step meetings where there would be a lot of people.

He and I discussed this. He understood the importance of the groups; that the people there and the information from the groups could help him learn how to stay sober. We devised a plan, however, allowing him to attend just two NA meetings each week (including finding a sponsor and talking to at least one person each meeting) while enhancing his recovery program through nature.

Makana wanted to become a better surfer, and wanted to plant and tend to a larger garden—one big enough to feed him. Both would take discipline, abstinence from drugs and, in Makana's view, respect for nature. He couldn't be a better surfer if he went into the water thinking he knew more about the ocean than the waves themselves. He had done that while high and almost got killed. He couldn't grow a decent garden unless he understood what would and wouldn't grow on his land; but he had always been too strung out to really do any learning about his soil. He knew some farmers and elders in his culture who could teach him. As it turned out, they also frequently asked him about his recovery. Learning from them and abiding by what he learned gave him sober options to his drug use and a deep respect for nature he didn't know was possible.

## Are Spiritual Sources of Support Okay?

Every time a reference to "God" appears in the original Twelve Steps, the recovery process in this book updates that term with "sources of support." Anything or anyone who can help you get and maintain sound judgment is a source of support for you.

"Wait!" you might say. "But I'm okay with the concept of God." If you are offended because you think this approach to recovery forces you to ignore God completely, remember that you are in charge of who you name as sources of support. As long as you name people or things that can help you maintain abstinence, you can name anyone or anything you want. If you believe in God, and God can help you remain abstinent, then use God as a part of this goal and this process.

Your sources of support could indeed *include* God or any spiritual influences. There are many possibilities for spiritual support, including:

- God

- Yahweh

- Jesus Christ

- Allah

- Buddha

- Vishnu

- Krishna

- Other religious figures, gods, or goddesses

Sources of support could also include people who are devoted to certain spiritual beings or religions. You could use them as sources of support as long as you can talk freely about your chemical dependency with them. Examples of spiritual leaders, teachers, masters, or teachings could include:

- Clergy, ministers

- Healers

- Shamans or holy people

- Writings or speeches by these sources

- Members of a church, synagogue, mosque, temple, dojo, or other spiritual or religious gathering

- Bhagavad Gita

- Tao Te Ching

- Confucianism

- Talmud

- Bible

- Koran

- Book of Mormon

- Book of Common Prayer

- Any other spiritual guide

## Group Support

Think seriously about including some sort of a group as a source of support. There are thousands of Alcoholics Anonymous and Narcotics Anonymous groups for alcohol and drug dependent people. Some areas have smaller but effective Twelve-Step groups. Check your phone book for groups like Marijuana Anonymous, Cocaine Anonymous, or Pills Anonymous. There are several hundred other groups in the United States that help members stay sober using the guidance of group support. Three other groups—Women for Sobriety, Secular Organizations for Sobriety, and Rational Recovery—provide an alternative to recovery without the Twelve Steps. You'll find a contact address for those groups in chapter 13.

Each recovery group has people who say the groups are helpful, and other people who say they are not. Some people will insist you go. Some will call you crazy if you do. However, you shouldn't decide whether or not a particular group will work for you until have attended at least *ten* sessions. Remember, you need to figure out for yourself what will help you. You'll shortchange yourself if you don't attend a group because of someone else's negative opinion. Discover on your own if a particular group could help you or not.

Did you include a group in your list of support? If not, think about this: People who attend some kind of support group have a better chance at staying abstinent than people who don't. It doesn't seem to matter what kind of group it is, just as long as they can talk about their chemical dependency and the need to stay abstinent. Find a group to use as a source of support to help you stay abstinent.

## Making Sure Your Sources of Support Can Really Help You

There is a limit, however, to what you should name as part of your sources of support. When you identify your sources of support, make sure at least half of them are living, adult human beings whom you can actually contact and talk with about your recovery. This might seem a ridiculous suggestion at first. None-theless, there's a point to it. You need personal, face-to-face guid-ance for your recovery. Distant people, deceased people, or nonliving characters are just not helpful for that kind of feedback. Some people, hoping to sneak by with an easy effort at recovery, name only sources of support that cannot give them face-to-face guidance, direction, and feedback. They do this because they don't really want to change their lives. They figure they can decide for themselves what these sources of support would probably tell them—and it may be something that won't even help them stay abstinent.

### Sources of Support to Avoid

Some chemically dependent people will choose celebrities, infant children, or historical figures to give them motivation and inspiration. However, when these chemically dependent people are nearing relapse, none of these inspiring figures can give face-to-face feedback for their recovery. Helen Keller, for example, may have overcome tremendous odds, but she cannot directly help you stay drug-free today. These intangible sources can be good addi-tions to your main sources of support like a therapist or a close friend, but they will not directly help you.

Other chemically dependent people try to avoid choosing hu-man sources of support and instead choose activities. Their hope is that a good job, more exercise, a healthy diet program, or a fun hobby will keep them too busy to use drugs or alcohol. This is a try at recovery by way of time management. If you want to avoid relapse, you'll need more feedback than you can get from your daily planner and a fiber bar. I have worked with dozens of re-lapsing hobbyists and marathon runners.

Some chemically dependent people say they will rely on God to help them stay sober. However, these people don't pray, attend church, read a holy book, or discuss religion with anyone. They, like those in the above examples, are doomed to relapse.

Kerin was a patient of mine who let me know in the first ses-sion that she was an addict, and also religious. When it came time to develop a list of sources of support, her list contained the fol-lowing: "God, Jesus, Holy Spirit, Virgin Mary, Saint Mary Mag-dela, my rosary, my priest, the Pope, the Bible and my church." I explained that she had set herself up—that out of her list, only her priest could possibly give her any face-to-face feedback, and he wouldn't be as available to her as she needed her support to be. She needed more sources of support who would be more accessible to her. Otherwise, I cautioned, she would relapse due to lack of support.

She responded angrily, saying I was antireligious. I asked her how she would handle some hypothetical situations like old friends looking her up, and she said prayer would be enough to keep her sober. I told her she needed to find at least four more sources of support who could give her more direct feedback. She refused, and said she was going to find a therapist who was sensitive to Christian issues. Two months later Kerin's name was in the paper, having been arrested on a drug-related charge.

Your nonhuman sources of support will certainly offer you some guidance and support. However, you will, at times, want to resist taking any advice and guidance. You could even want to claim that a source of support—which no one but you can understand—actually guided you into relapse.

You need as much definite, certain guidance as you can get. You need contact with people or things that can help you become abstinent and warn you when you're heading toward relapse. Therefore, make sure half your sources of support can talk with you face-to-face, or at least on the phone. Make sure they can listen to your concerns and offer you advice that you'll understand clearly, even if you aren't happy with the good advice that you get.

## What to Expect From Your Sources of Support

Remember that the sources of support you identify are only supposed to help you to overcome your chemical dependency. They might not be so hot at helping you with other problems in your life. Someone who can give you good advice about stopping your drug use may not provide the best advise about how to prepare your income tax. Someone at a support-group meeting who may understand your problems with alcohol dependency may not offer the best advice for your concerns about your relationships. An inspirational book or pamphlet that helps educate you about withdrawal symptoms may not give helpful hints when you try to decide how to discipline your child.

Your sources of support will help you in many ways, but always in how to stay abstinent. They will help you begin abstinence and give you advice, encouragement, feedback, and guidance.

For now, you should just work on starting your abstinence and recovery. Eventually, you may make important life decisions that both affect your recovery and help you to maintain your abstinence. The time may come for you to make more serious lifestyle changes, like marriage, divorce, return to school, change of job, or moving. When the time comes for you to make these kinds of major life changes, you will have your sources of support in place and make the decisions best with the help of people and things that will support your abstinence.

## Making Your List

Name at least ten sources of support that could help you get and stay abstinent. Write down the names, things, objects, titles, and ideas you can use to help you. Write down your list of sources of support on a piece of paper or in your journal.

The people you choose as your sources of support should be able to discuss your recovery with you. They should truly respect your responsibility for recovery, especially if you name a professional. You could also use someone such as a member of a recovery support group who you respect. Make sure you also write down how each source of support can help you stay abstinent. As you think about who or what could be a source of support for you, consider the following questions. Include your answers as part of your list, either on the following page or on your separate list.

- **How will you use each source of support?** Every name that goes on your list needs an explanation. For example, if you say "My Friend Nick," then how will you use Nick's help? Will you get help through Nick's own experience, or will Nick just be a supportive voice on the phone?

- **How will you know when each source of support works for you?** Explain how you expect your abstinence will be helped by your sources. Will they help you avoid thinking about opportunities to use? Will they occupy your free time? How will you make them become a crucial part of your ability to avoid drugs or alcohol?

- **How will you know if a source of support doesn't work?** How long will you wait to get results from a source? What if the results aren't what you expected? What will you do to "retire" a source if it proves to actually encourage you to relapse rather than abstain?

- **What will you do to get the most out of each source of support you name?** How often will you contact each source? Will your contact usually be face-to-face or by phone? What kinds of questions will you ask so you make sure you understand what they recommend to you?

## *Identify Sources of Support*

Here are the names of at least ten people and things—my sources of support—I can count on to help me choose not to use drugs or drink alcohol, and the ways I can rely on their help. The more detailed and honest your answers, the more likely that each source of support can help you. The more your sources help you the more likely your future recovery will succeed.

| Source of Support | How This Source of Support Can Help Me Stay Abstinent |
|---|---|
| 1. | |
| 2. | |
| 3. | |
| 4. | |
| 5. | |
| 6. | |

7. _____     _____

     _____     _____

8. _____     _____

     _____     _____

9. _____     _____

     _____     _____

10. _____     _____

     _____     _____

# Discuss Your List
# with Someone

If you want to get the most out of this goal, then you should discuss your work on this goal with at least one person. Use this person's feedback to help you make sure that your list of sources of support is solid and useful to you. This person will probably be one of the sources of support you name on your list. When you review your list, make sure you've avoided people who may not be able to help you the way you need to be helped—a casual acquaintance, a loved one who's been begging you to get help, or a therapist or counselor unfamiliar with recovery. These people, while probably well intended, may not understand the full nature of chemical dependency, recovery, abstinence, and the work you will need to do to achieve it.

Don't cut corners with your recovery. That trusted other, especially a counselor or therapist, will need to ask you to explain your choices of sources of support. Be ready. You might become angry and react defensively when they do this. Remember what you have learned so far: You have set up your lifestyle so you could use drugs or drink alcohol, and you don't trust authority figures or anyone who could get in the way of your using or drinking. Someone who asks you to explain your sources of support will probably stir up some anxiety in you. However, a counselor or trusted other who questions your work on this goal will not do this to threaten you, but to encourage you to explain how it will work. You want a list that you can rely on for help when you need it, so it's important to make sure you have the right people and things on it.

For example, a patient of mine named Adam had included on his list his probation officer and his ex-girlfriend. He included his PO, he said, because the PO could motivate him with the threat of jail if Adam used drugs again. However, Adam hated his PO, and never referred to him without including profanity in the description. His ex could motivate him he claimed, because she said she might get back together with him if he got sober. Now, however, he thought she was dating another man.

Rather than a help to his recovery, both these people were more likely potential sources of blame by Adam for a relapse. After some discussion with me and a group of other addicts, Adam realized it was his desire to avoid jail, and not his PO, that was his real source of support. Adam agreed to drop his ex's name from the list too, since he knew he wouldn't be able to trust her help. He didn't trust her at all, in fact.

Pamela, a patient in another group, also needed the opportunity to discuss her list with someone. She had thought for a week about who she would include, but said she could only come up with two names. The other members in the group reminded her of the names of people she had mentioned while in the group. One support-group member had even seen her in the community with a few people who "looked nice." Pamela agreed they would be helpful to her recovery. It took only twenty minutes for Pamela to have a list of eight people, a book, a church, and two different support groups to help her with her recovery. She couldn't have completed her list, however, without the help of someone.

## Using Your List: Discussing Your Recovery with Someone

Now actually use your list—discuss your situation with a few of those trusted others. You'll get much needed support as you begin to enact your program of recovery. People on your list may already know of your problem. Tell them you are beginning to work on a solution. Tell them that you might suffer some withdrawal symptoms and be in a bad mood for a few days. Then, and most importantly, ask for their help and support. Perhaps they could call and check up on you or spend some time with you. Maybe they can just ask you how things are going when they see you. They won't do anything for you if you do not talk with them first.

## Reaching Your Second Goal

Your second goal helps you identify sources of support that can help you get abstinent, stay abstinent, and restore sound judgment to your life. The therapeutic statement for this goal reads:

> *I name certain people and things besides myself which could help me restore sound judgment to my life.*

You need to stay abstinent if you want to overcome the chemical dependency. Remember, you diagnosed yourself with the first goal; now you have one more goal to complete before you begin the real work toward recovery. You must make a commitment to do the work.

# 3

Make a Commitment to Work toward Change

To recover from chemical dependency, you have to change your current lifestyle to one that will support your abstinence. With the guidance and help of the sources of support you identified in the second goal you'll make lifestyle changes. This third goal will help you make a commitment to use your sources of support in order to make the lifestyle changes *last*.

In the third step, AA members declare their willingness to change: "Made a decision to turn our will and our lives over to the care of God *as we understood Him*." Let's look at what this means for you, and how it applies to your third goal.

## Decision

When you *decide* something, you make up your mind and resolve yourself to some course of action. This is an important step for you. With this goal, you'll make up your mind to commit to the work it takes to recover from chemical dependency.

The process offered in this book will help you become abstinent from drugs and alcohol. So, this commitment has to do with making up your mind to do whatever is necessary to allow you to stay abstinent and commit to the goals. Read on.

## "Our Will and Our Lives"

Your *will* is your *wish* or *desire*. Your *life*, means, of course, your day-to-day existence. These two terms, together, mean more than just being alive. These terms now refer to all the things you might want, or wish, to do in your day-to-day living.

Your daily life gives you opportunities to make decisions. A lot of those decisions have to do with whether or not you will use drugs or alcohol. These three concepts together refer to a commitment you make regarding your *day-to-day decision-making around drugs and alcohol.* Pay attention to how the following concepts build on this commitment.

## "Turn Over"

For the purposes of this process of recovery, *turn over* means to "seek guidance." Using this process, you won't just hand over your wants and desires to any old person or thing. You will seek guidance in your day-to-day living to help you maintain your abstinence. Now, from whom or from where will you seek that guidance?

## "God as We Understood Him"

In the third step, the word *God* refers to the same thing identified in the second step as a *Power*—that is, God is a source of support for AA members. When you completed your second goal, you defined this therapeutic concept for yourself when you made up your list of sources of support.

In the 1930s, when the Twelve Steps were written, American culture related to God differently than it does today. A commitment to God was seen as essential for recovery from an alcohol problem. For that reason, the Steps refer to "God" or to "Him" five different times. For the purposes of this therapeutic process, beginning with this goal, the terms God, *God as we understood Him*, or *Him*, will simply be replaced by your list of sources of support.

Your sources of support will help you stay in charge of your recovery. Whatever or whoever can help you become and remain abstinent is a source of support for you, whether or not you choose to include *God* in that list.

## Wrapping it All Up: Your Commitment to Work toward Change

The idea behind this third goal is this: You must make a commitment to seek guidance from your sources of support whenever you want to do something in your day-to-day living that could affect your recovery. Reaching this goal will keep you abstinent.

All this talk about commitment might make you—the nervous beginner to recovery—worry about giving up control of your life. That's a natural response. Just remember that the only thing you're giving up is your efforts to try to control your use of drugs and alcohol. If you're still concerned, just keep in mind that if you could have controlled your drug and alcohol use, you would have done so already without outside help. When you made your self-diagnosis, you admitted you don't have that kind of control.

You should understand that your work in this goal is as permanent as your chemical dependency. It starts the process of changing your lifestyle. If you want to stay in charge of your life, you need to accept the responsibility to make your abstinence a priority. Whenever you don't know how to maintain your abstinence, you need to check things out with a source of support. In this chapter, you will learn how to recognize the times that you'll need to ask for help from your support.

Right now, you may not always know whether or not decisions in your life could affect your abstinence. That's why you need to be in frequent contact with some of your sources of support, for now. When you get in the habit of seeking guidance for your abstinence, you also get in the habit of remaining abstinent.

It may seem odd, but by giving up trying to control your use of drugs and alcohol, you actually take charge of that part of your life. You'll never lose control of your drug use or drinking once you decide to stop trying to control your drug use and drinking. By using your sources of support, you can learn how to stay abstinent. By staying abstinent, you'll get back your sound judgment.

If you do that, you can get back all the control over your life that you had lost because of your drug or alcohol use. Once you've accomplished that, there's no end to what improvements and changes you'll make in your life as a recovering person.

# When to Seek Support

When you face a decision, however, that could threaten your ability to stay abstinent, then you must seek guidance from your sources of support. This will help you make the best decision—the one that will help you remain abstinent. Here are some examples showing what it means to realize you need some support to maintain recovery.

### A Wedding Invitation

Suppose you have made a self-diagnosis as having alcohol dependency and you've started recovery. You have stayed alcohol-free for a few rewarding weeks. Today you've been invited to a relative's wedding; it's a month from now. The problem? Your family is famous for throwing boozy receptions after anyone gets married. The last time there was a wedding the bride and groom hired cabs to come at the end of the reception to take everyone home because they knew there wouldn't be enough sober drivers to go around.

Based on the first three goals, your situation looks like this: First, you have admitted that you cannot always predict how much you will drink, or what might happen when you choose to drink. Second, you have identified several sources of support that can help you avoid making the choice to drink. Third, you've made a commitment to use these sources of support for just such an occasion as this one.

You're now faced with a dilemma that could lead you to relapse, to start drinking again. So, now you should seek the guidance of your sources of support. Talk with them about this situation. Give them all the details, and discuss your options. You know that you would face an awful lot of risk if you went.

- Would it be wiser for you to just attend the wedding ceremony, and not attend the reception but send a nice gift?

- Could you take a guest, someone who you knew wouldn't drink and who wouldn't encourage you to drink either?

- Do you really need to go to this wedding?

After all this discussion, you should use their advice to help you make the healthiest decision, a decision that will keep you abstinent. What is the healthiest thing for you to do, at this point, with only a couple of months of abstinence behind you?

## Getting Together with Old Friends

Suppose you have a drug addiction. You have admitted that when you use your drug, you cannot predict how much you will use, nor what will be the consequences of your use. Tonight, after four weeks of abstinence, you have the opportunity to go to someone's house and get together with some people you haven't seen since you started recovery to watch someone's home video of a recent vacation.

Now that you're already into your third goal, you have some sources of support with whom you can discuss your decision. Call them up and talk about this decision you need to make. You should do this before you make the decision of whether or not to go.

Here are some bases to cover with your sources of support:

- When was the last time you got together with these people and did *not* use drugs?

- What are the chances that they're actually going to watch a video, as opposed to breaking out some alcohol or drugs and partying-down?

- How realistic is it to think that you can be around people who use drugs or drink alcohol and not use or drink yourself?

- How open will these people be if you want to bring a drug-free friend along?

- How open will these old friends be to the fact that you're drug-free?

Now, having discussed these points, make a decision. What is the healthiest, safest, protects-my-recovery-the-most decision you can make?

## A Memorial Service

How about this: You have begun recovery from chemical dependency. You've accepted that you cannot control how much you will use or what will happen if you choose to use. It's been six months now, and you're proud of your abstinence. Today you get a phone call from a former drug-using companion who tells you that someone you considered a good friend while you were using died two days ago. The memorial service will happen this weekend, at a bar. It's time to call a source of support, or two, and talk about your options.

- Is a bar a safe place for you to be?
- Even if you didn't drink alcohol regularly, have you drunk when your drug-of-choice wasn't around?
- Will people probably bring other drugs anyway?
- Will the people there respect your abstinence?
- Could some people there look at you as an outsider, or a betrayer, and give you a hard time?
- The emotions will run high at this memorial service; have you ever experienced such strong emotions without using or drinking?
- What was your relationship with this person like after you started your recovery?
- Was this person such a good friend that you really should go to the service and risk your abstinence?

You have several choices. Should you go with someone else? Stay only a short time? Don't go, send flowers, and write a letter to your buddy's family?

## Going Out on a First Date

Say you've been practicing your program of recovery for four good months. You feel great; you've even got some self-confidence you'd forgotten you could feel. Today after one of your support-group meetings, another member suggested the two of you should go out for coffee sometime soon. You said you'd think about it. The biggest problem that you can think of is that dating has always made you nervous, and being nervous has always been something you claimed made you want to drink or use drugs. You try to tell yourself that "going out for coffee" isn't the same thing as "going out on a date," but it doesn't sound true. Time to call a source of support. Maybe it's time to call several of them. You need to discuss whether or not this is safe for you to do.

- Recovery is challenging enough right now; should you really be thinking about how to get back into dating too?

- Have you ever dated and not felt like wanting to use or drink? If dating has always made you nervous, shouldn't you work on this with a professional, or as part of your recovery program before taking the plunge again?

- Doesn't it seem risky to date someone in your support group? What if things get messy—will you be obligated to stop going to the group?

- This other person knows you're relatively new to the program, and still unsure about a lot of things. Could it be you're being seen as a target for something more than just coffee?

You've got three basic choices that you should discuss with a source of support. You could go. You could not go. You could get a group together to go with the two of you. What makes the most sense in the long run for your recovery?

In each of these four examples, you would do the same thing. You would decide with the help of your sources of support whether or not you should go at all, and under what conditions. By sticking to these goals, you have an excellent chance of maintaining your abstinence no matter what decision you make. You could discuss strategies if you decide to go, and alternatives if you decide not to go.

It might seem hard to stick to this goal in the beginning. It can be difficult to come face-to-face with the true nature of making lifestyle changes. Change is hard but necessary if you want to regain your sound judgment. Consider again the examples of the wedding reception, "the old gang," the memorial service, and the date. In each situation, your wisest decision would be to not participate in any of those events. Maybe in your future you could survive such risks, but not as early in your recovery as the examples suggest.

### *Think of an Example of Your Own*

Think of a situation in your own life where you will need to seek support from your sources. Imagine a situation that might give you the opportunity to drink alcohol or use drugs. Do you have an invitation you're considering? Is there a special event coming up? How about your birthday? Is there a holiday soon? Do you live or work near people or places where you can get drugs or alcohol? Are you coming into money soon?

In these situations, do you know how to avoid drug or alcohol use? You should discuss the situation and your options with one or more of your sources of support. How will you do that? By phone? In person? What kind of support will you want from them? Should they listen to your options, or help you brainstorm different solutions? How can they help you make the healthiest decision possible? Are you beginning to see how this process works? You should get used to doing this whenever you make decisions that could affect your recovery. That way it will become automatic for you to learn how to protect your abstinence in your day-to-day decision-making.

## Are You Ready to Proceed?

With this third goal, you make a commitment to do the work necessary to begin and maintain your abstinence and recovery. This is a personal decision. You need to have an honest conversation with one of your sources of support. Try talking with that person who helped you review your second goal list of sources of support.

You need to commit to a permanent change in your behavior—seeking guidance to help you abstain from your drug or alcohol use. When you can make a commitment to follow the guidance of your sources of support in order to help you maintain abstinence, you have completed your third goal.

By doing this, you can work more successfully at making your life as you would rather have it: predictable and manageable, keeping you in charge.

## Reaching Your Third Goal

The therapeutic statement for this goal reads:

> *I commit to seek guidance from those sources of support in my day-to-day decision-making.*

The commitment you make with this goal begins to blend with the work of the next one. In the fourth goal, you begin to examine your lifestyle for relapse-prone and abstinence-supporting behavior.

# 4

## Examine and Discuss Your Lifestyle

It's time now to figure out what it is about your life that allows you to go back to drinking or drug use, even after you have decided not to do it anymore. If you want to maintain abstinence, you must learn how to prevent relapse. Your fourth goal will help you examine how your lifestyle allows you both to abstain and to relapse. To do this, you need to make a thorough examination of your lifestyle. Once you get an idea of how your lifestyle supports your drug or alcohol use, you can put yourself in charge of making changes for the better.

This goal uses the concepts from the fourth and fifth steps of Alcoholics Anonymous, which help AA members start the actual work of changing their lives. This goal will help you continue with the changes you've already begun to make. Let's start by taking a look at the terms used in the original fourth step: "Made a searching and fearless moral inventory of ourselves." (The fifth step concept will be discussed near the end of this chapter.)

## "A Searching and Fearless Inventory of Ourselves"

The word *searching* means "examining carefully or thoroughly," and *fearless* means "courageous." *Inventory,* for the purposes of this recovery process, refers to another list that you will make with this goal. You will make it carefully and courageously. Now, what is that list about?

The word *ourselves* in the fourth step keeps the focus on you. When you make your list, you should keep the focus on yourself. As noted in chapters 2 and 3, the work you do for your recovery must focus on you and on your own behavior and lifestyle, not someone else's. While you work on this goal, you'll take an honest look at some of the ways you've created problems yourself. That kind of examination won't be easy. It's humbling and sometimes embarrassing work. You'll find yourself inclined to justify your past behavior, blame it on someone else or on uncontrollable circumstances. That kind of rationalization is a way to make yourself feel better when working on this list makes you uncomfortable: *blaming someone else keeps your focus off you.* That won't help you finish this process, or improve your chances for lasting recovery. Later on in this chapter, you'll see how you should check your work with someone else to help you keep the focus on yourself. Doing that will better your chances for abstinence and recovery.

For now, working on this goal, you will make a careful, thorough list about yourself, without fearing what you might find. However, what exactly do you search for? The fourth step calls for AA members to search their *moral* character.

## Moral

*Moral,* as it is used in the fourth step, pertains "to or is concerned with right conduct or the distinction between right and wrong." While that definition works well for a spiritual program of recovery like AA, this therapeutic process uses a different interpretation of the word. "The distinction between right and wrong" can mean many different things. A child can learn the difference between right and wrong, and then learn how to behave properly.

A person with chemical dependency, however, has a health matter to contend with, not a moral issue. Chemically dependent people need to learn more than just a simple understanding of the difference between right and wrong. You need to know the difference between what is healthy and unhealthy. For a person recovering from drug or alcohol dependency, the difference between right and wrong means the difference between what helps you abstain (that's healthy) and what helps you relapse (that's unhealthy).

In order to recover from chemical dependency, you need to learn the difference between the things you do which help you remain abstinent, and the things you do which will lead you to relapse. Know this, and you can know how to recover. For this goal, you will make a list of the ways you behave leading you to relapse and the ways you behave supporting your abstinence. For this process of recovery, that is all there is to the concept of the difference between right and wrong.

# Keeping It Simple: Relapse and Abstinence

If you had hoped for a broader, more thorough examination of your life, please keep this in mind: At this point in the process, you should only examine your lifestyle characteristics having to do with relapse and abstinence. Of course you have other issues in your life that you may want to examine or talk about. You'll have the chance to address those other issues as part of the last three goals of this process. For now, just wait. This is important for a few reasons.

Too often, chemically dependent people who are new to recovery try to do too much too soon. In these cases, they try to tackle emotional issues as well as the chemical dependency. The danger in doing this is that you can lose sight of your recovery. You might, unknowingly, set yourself up to relapse by not paying enough attention to your recovery—it's happened to many people.

Right now, don't explore any deeply personal, criminal, or disgraceful things that you might have done. It's too soon for you to examine your self-esteem, relationships, family of origin issues, sexual assault, career goals, parenting skills, or other secondary recovery issues.

Dealing with everything at once is too overwhelming; this is how your attention will get distracted from learning how to remain abstinent. You'll only relapse.

At this point in your recovery, you'll probably feel insecure, vulnerable, and fragile. You're changing your lifestyle, after all; a lifestyle you've lived for some time and gotten used to. You don't have the ability yet to successfully explore emotionally traumatic issues, as well as focus on your recovery.

As you work on recovery, you'll find your private and emotional life improving naturally. However, forcing this to happen before its time shouldn't be your first priority. You will work on other areas in your life later on, when you have a better chance of working on them successfully. As you succeed in your recovery, you'll gain a sense of ability, accomplishment, and higher self-esteem. The lifestyle that you have to set up to avoid relapse will also support you when the time comes to deal with those other more emotional issues. Again, however, that time is not now. Be patient.

For now, start to examine your lifestyle.

## Looking at the Healthy and Unhealthy Aspects of Your Lifestyle

To help you reach this goal, you'll make a list of your lifestyle characteristics that allow you to relapse, then make another list of characteristics that allow you to stay abstinent. You need to make a thorough and courageous list. This involves looking at both sides of the issue.

You shouldn't examine just those lifestyle characteristics that allow you to relapse like hanging out with drug users or going to liquor stores. By just changing your unhealthy lifestyle characteristics, you'll only create a void. Yes, you can identify and remove a lot of your trouble, but what happens then? What will fill all that empty space left over in your life?

A patient of mine, Liz, created problems for herself by focusing only on her unhealthy characteristics. She found it easy to admit to having an addiction. When she went to support groups she spent a lot of time describing the ways she neglected her children, let her parents and husband down, and had destroyed friendships. Some people in the groups admired her honesty. Liz, however, began to feel more and more hopeless. After five months attending meetings, she didn't feel she had made any real progress. Yes, she was abstinent, but she thought she'd feel better once she got abstinent. All she was doing at the meetings was focusing on what an awful addict she had been. It wasn't very satisfying for her.

Everett had a similar problem. Everett had the good fortune of being rather successful despite his alcohol problem. He began treatment reluctantly, but thought he had the hang of it after a few weeks. Everett focused on the problems he had created in his life, and on the amount of work he had yet to do in order to gain more time in recovery. He expressed a lot of dissatisfaction in himself throughout recovery, and a lot of impatience with how long it was taking. Several of his peers in group sessions tried to give him encouragement for the things he had going for him, and the things he had done to get as far along in recovery as he had. However, Everett always argued his own points, never letting anyone talk him out of them.

Both Everett and Liz began to question whether or not they wanted to continue with recovery. They both focused so much on the negative that both actually forgot to bring anything positive to their recovery. They were only looking at one side of their issue. By focusing only on the unhealthy and not replacing that with anything healthy, both created a void that didn't make recovery seem that attractive.

A member of Liz's group pulled her aside after one meeting and suggested Liz was being too hard on herself. Liz and this other member spoke over coffee about the attributes in Liz's life. Liz admitted she had made progress in the five months she'd stayed away from drugs. She acknowledged that her recovery was making her a better mother, wife, and daughter, and that she wanted to improve on those characteristics even more. She recognized she had been an inspiration to other members in the group, even just by virtue of the fact she'd been a regular face at the meeting, helping to give the meeting a sense of cohesion and stability. After that conversation, Liz told me she made a promise to herself to say one positive thing about herself for every negative thing. After a while, though she never lost sight of the fact that she was in recovery permanently, she spoke almost always about the positive things she was accomplishing.

Everett also decided to stop being so hard on himself. He was startled when, during a group session, the entire group groaned when he began one of his self-loathing comments. That caught his attention, and he listened as each member of the group reported that he had become a liability to the group. It was hard to feel sorry for a self-proclaimed loser making a quarter of a million dollars a year, and even harder to get inspiration from him. No one wanted him to continue with the group if he couldn't improve his focus. Everett was embarrassed, and he vowed to improve his attitude. Beginning at the next group he talked about the progress he was making in taking care of the problems his alcohol dependency had created, how proud he felt of his accomplishments, and—most significantly to the group—he began each session announcing how many days it had been since his last drink. As his focus improved, his progress through these goals sped up.

If you don't fill that void with something healthy, you'll eventually relapse. That is why you need to list the things you have done in your past that have allowed you to be able to abstain. Those are your healthy strengths.

## Calling On Your Hidden Strengths—Healthy and Unhealthy

Before you began this process of recovery, there were times when you chose to not use drugs or alcohol. You have, maybe even frequently, resisted the urges and opportunities to use or drink. Maybe you resisted because of a lack of time or money, because of possible consequences, because of personal pride, or even just sheer white-knuckled willpower. You probably resisted as a result of some temporary attitude adjustment and behavior changes that you imposed on yourself. The point is, you *have* abstained at times in your past.

The fact that you are capable of avoiding drug or alcohol use, for a while at least, is important. If you can figure out how you do it for a short time, then you can use that skill to do it permanently. This goal helps you figure out what exactly your skills are. Later, when you work on your sixth goal, you'll build on these particular characteristics to make them a stronger influence in your life.

However, like every chemically dependent person, you've also always known how to set yourself up to drink or use again. This doesn't mean you have known simply how to make yourself a drink or use a drug. This means you have known how set yourself up to *get* your drink or drug. When you have wanted to drink or use, you've known just who to call, where to go, what to do, or what events to set in motion to allow the opportunity to come up. You know what it takes to get what you've needed. Knowing this about yourself is important too. If you can figure out how you relapse, then you can figure out how to avoid relapsing. You'll also do some work to avoid these characteristics in your sixth goal.

# High-Risk Characteristics

To work on reaching this goal, think about how you set yourself up for relapse. Soon you'll be asked to write examples of how you do this. You relapse because you engage in *high-risk* activities. Something is high risk if it sets you up to use drugs or drink alcohol. High-risk activities include a variety of thoughts, attitudes, or behaviors.

## *High-Risk Thoughts*

A thought can be high risk if it helps you set yourself up to use or drink. High-risk thoughts are often mind games—or rationalizations—you play with yourself. You use these games to help rationalize using or drinking again. Read the following examples of high-risk thoughts and think about how many different times you've thought to yourself:

- I'll use just this one time. I can get away with it.

- I'll only use a little bit.

- I will use (or drink) so carefully this time that I won't have any problems.

- I can use or drink and no one will find out.

- My problem is just with this one drug, so I can use this other drug, because I don't really have a problem with it.

- If I go to the party, I'm sure that all the active addicts there will respect my decision not to use anymore.

- I know drugs have caused me nothing but trouble, but I still don't think I'm really chemically dependent.

- I have to drink green beer—it's St. Patrick's Day.

- I'll only spend this much, then I won't use too much.

- Gee, that's a new drug, I wonder what getting high with that drug would be like?

- I have to drink or use drugs. It's part of my nationality.

- I want to help her get sober, but the only way she'll listen to me is if I get high too.

- If I take a cab home, then it'll be okay if I drink. That shows I'm responsible.

- I'll use, but I won't let the kids see me. They'll never know.

- I wonder if my drug-using friends still hang out at this place? Would it really hurt to just go and say "hello" to be sociable?

- I'm just gonna use or drink, and I won't even let myself think about it.

## High-Risk Attitudes

Attitudes can also be high risk. You experience high-risk attitudes usually as part of a reaction to something that makes you feel negative, or at least something other than positive. That is, anything that bums you out, irritates you, or makes you forget about the positive things in your life makes you prone to high-risk attitudes. A high-risk attitude puts you in a frame of mind that lets you justify giving up on your commitment to abstain. Think about how many different times you've felt some way that made you say to yourself things like:

- My boss was riding me all day—I deserve a drink.

- Yay! My team won! I'm going to celebrate with a cold beer. Everyone else is.

- Aww! My team lost! I'm going to console myself with a joint.

- If she'd keep the house clean I wouldn't have to relax myself with drugs before I went home.

- Those darn kids are driving me crazy. I need something to help calm my nerves.

- I have to use drugs or drink in my line of work.

- I have to use if I want to be accepted in this group.

- I had a lousy childhood. That's why I use.

- Boy, do I hate arguing. I need something to help me relax.

- I've been abstinent for so long I'm sure I could use or drink again, and it won't be a problem.

- I'm fat—I need to use this to help me lose weight.

- I need to increase my energy and stamina. I'll use this.

- This doesn't really count as a drug because it's a natural herb. It should be legal, after all.

- We all have to die from something.

- The world sucks. Why should I stay clearheaded for that?

- Famous people in history have used drugs. Why can't I?

- Everyone in this room is using and drinking but me. I feel really out of place. I'm just not the type of person who can talk to everyone, I need an icebreaker.

- Why does everyone always get on my case? Why doesn't anyone ever say anything about that other person's problems? I've got twice the amount of pressure—I can't handle it without a drink.

- I hate spending time with my parents. They always treat me like I'm still a baby. I know! I'll bring a bottle along to help keep me calm.

## High-Risk Behaviors

All chemically dependent people behave in ways that are high risk. These might be the easiest high-risk tendencies to recognize. High-risk behaviors are the many things you actually do to set yourself up to drink or use. High-risk attitudes and high-risk thoughts often come in combination for recovering chemically dependent people. Usually, a high-risk thought springs from a high-risk attitude. That can give you all the reason you need to engage in a high-risk behavior. Think of how many different times you have done the following:

- Bought drugs or alcohol

- Bought drugs or alcohol even if you didn't plan to use or drink

- Walked down a street where you knew drugs were sold

- Went anyplace where you knew drugs or alcohol would be available

- Avoided people who would tell you to abstain

- Put extra money in your pocket "just to have"

- Accepted an invitation to do something where you knew drugs would be available

- Refused to accept an invitation because you knew you wouldn't be able to drink or use at the event

- Spent time with certain people who use or drink—knowing that the only time you ever spend with them is when you want to use or drink

- Kept in touch with using or drinking buddies, even when you were trying to quit

- Lied to friends, family, or your children when they asked about your drug or alcohol use

- Started a fight with someone so you could blame them for your using or drinking

- Let people call you by a nickname that you earned while drinking or using drugs

- Wore drug or alcohol slogans on your clothes

- Encouraged someone else to start using drugs or alcohol

- Made arrangements so you could use drugs or alcohol without having to worry so much about the consequences

# Low-Risk Characteristics

Now you need to think about what lifestyle characteristics of yours have kept you abstinent in your past or even now. These characteristics are *low-risk* thoughts, attitudes, and behaviors because when you do them, your risk for relapse is low. Understanding this part of yourself will help you to abstain for good.

## *Low-Risk Thoughts*

Low-risk thoughts are the things you say to yourself that help you choose to stay away from opportunities to use or to drink. These thoughts usually show you have the ability to think ahead. They show that you either really want to avoid relapse, or that you want to avoid the consequences that could come if you use or drink again. They're healthy thoughts that help you make healthy decisions and protect your abstinence. Think of the times you've said the following things to yourself:

- Nah, I don't think I will.

- If I do that, I'll probably lose something important to me.

- I know if I go to that place tonight I won't be able to resist the offers to use or drink. So I won't go.

- I know I'll get into trouble if I use or drink, so I won't.

- Boy, do I hate looking that goofy when I use. No thanks.

- Every time I go there, I end up getting high or drunk. I think I won't go there this time.

- He's a nice guy, but every time I see him, he's sucking on a beer. I think I won't spend any one-on-one time with him.

- I might be able to get away with using or drinking. On the other hand, I'll bet I'll have to give a urine sample for a drug test at work soon, or one for my probation officer. So I better not use or drink.

- My partner and I get along so much better since I stopped using. I think I'll keep things the way they are.

- My children don't seem so upset since I stopped drinking. I think I'll keep things the way they are.

- My partner told me the last time I got high that it was either stay abstinent or get lost. I think I'd rather stay with my partner.

- I never got a promotion back in my drinking and using days. I think I could do it now, if I just stay abstinent.

- If I hadn't been using, I wouldn't have had that accident. I don't think I want to go through that again.

- Treatment was so expensive, I'd hate to waste all that money. I'd also hate to spend it all again on another treatment episode.

## Low-Risk Attitudes

You experience low-risk attitudes when you feel positive, confident (but not too confident). Low-risk attitudes put you in a frame of mind that helps you keep yourself abstinent. Your abstinence isn't in jeopardy when you have low-risk attitudes. Think of the times you have felt good enough to say the following things:

- Jeez, I've already had enough of that junk to last me a lifetime.

- I want more out of my life than I'm going to get if I do drugs or drink.

- I really don't need to use or drink.

- I'm really a happier person when I don't use.

- I can't be a good parent using or drinking, so I won't.

- I like the way people treat me when I don't use or drink.

- I'll show them they were wrong to think I couldn't stay abstinent.

- I'd rather be a good influence on my kids than a bad one.

- I'm glad I can go through a week without having to apologize for something I did when I was drunk or high.

- The boss seems to be trusting me more now that I've been abstinent for a while. This is great!

- Wow, ever since I stopped using drugs, nicer kinds of single, eligible people are interested in going out with me. I like that.

- It's a relief that people aren't so afraid of me anymore.

- I actually have some money saved in the bank because I'm not blowing it on drugs or alcohol. I wonder how long it would take me to double my savings.

- I think I could go back to school now that I've let my brain clear for a while.

- I'd like to be someone other people could look up to. If I stay abstinent, I could be that kind of person.

## Low-Risk Behaviors

Low-risk behaviors are the things you do to help you stay drug- or alcohol-free. Low-risk behaviors aren't just doing the opposite of high-risk behaviors, they're independent things you do that help you stay abstinent and help you increase your chances of staying abstinent in the future. Low-risk behaviors come from maintaining low-risk attitudes and thoughts. Again, think of how often you have:

- Chosen to make friends who don't use

- Made arrangements to spend time with people who don't use or drink

- Hung out with people who never encourage you to use or drink

- Given control of your money to someone else, or made a choice to switch your paycheck to direct deposit so you won't carry around big chunks of money

- Chosen to spend time at certain places where you wouldn't be able to use or drink

- Gotten rid of your stash of drugs, or gave away your liquor supply (including ALL that beer you bought on sale)

- Attended some kind of group or activity which would help you avoid drugs or alcohol

- Said "no" to an invitation to an event where you knew you could get drugs or alcohol

- Volunteered with a group or activity to keep your time occupied and free from drug- or alcohol-using activities

- Talked, honestly, with someone you respected about your drug or alcohol use and how you wanted to quit and stay quit

- Honestly helped someone else stay away from drugs or alcohol

- Talked with a doctor or dentist about your chemical dependency before you got a prescription you didn't have to have

# Making Your Lists

Either in your journal, in this book, or on two separate pieces of paper, you'll create two different lists. They will look like the ones on the following pages, only you will write from your own experience. Make your lists thorough. Carefully think about what you write down. These lists will be an important part of your recovery in future goal-work.

## *Your High-Risk Thoughts, Attitudes, and Behaviors*

On your first list, write down at least ten examples of thoughts, attitudes, and behaviors you have used to set yourself up to relapse. Write down these examples. Challenge yourself to think about many different times. Be specific: name names, give dates, write down the dollar amounts. Review the previous examples and answer these questions:

- How have you gotten hold of your drugs or alcohol?

- What are the names of the people who you have known to call or visit to get hold of drugs or alcohol?

- Where have you gone to get drugs or alcohol?

- During what kinds of events have you almost always used or drank?

- What have you known to do so that you could use or drink within the next few days?

- What have you said or done to other people in your life to keep them off your back?

- What kinds of stress have you said caused your use of drugs or alcohol?

- How have you given yourself permission to be involved in high-risk situations?

- What are the ways (or behaviors) in which you have used other people to help you get or use drugs or alcohol— whether these people knew they were helping you or not?

- What kinds of thoughts have you had that convinced you to use drugs or alcohol?

- What kinds of attitudes usually make you want to use or drink?

Write down your lifestyle characteristics that have helped you relapse. It's only natural to feel embarrassed by some of your examples. However, you can probably write down enough examples of high-risk thoughts, attitudes, and behaviors without having to include extremely private, criminal, or socially repulsive things. If you have thought, felt, or behaved in a way that helped you to decide to use or drink again and again, then write it down.

## Examining Your Lifestyle—High-Risk Thoughts, Attitudes, and Behaviors

Write five examples of thoughts, five attitudes, and ten behaviors you have used to make it possible for you to drink alcohol or use drugs. (It is often easier for people to think of their behaviors, which is why I have suggested writing only five examples of thoughts and attitudes.)

1. _____
2. _____
3. _____
4. _____
5. _____
6. _____
7. _____
8. _____
9. _____
10. _____
11. _____
12. _____
13. _____
14. _____
15. _____
16. _____
17. _____
18. _____
19. _____
20. _____

## Low-Risk Thoughts, Attitudes, and Behaviors

Now on to your second list. On your next page, make a list of at least twenty thoughts, attitudes, and behaviors that you have used to help keep yourself from using or drinking. Challenge yourself just as thoroughly with this list as you did with the other. Think long and hard about the things you have thought, felt, and done. You can review the low-risk characteristics section as a reminder of what they are. To make your list, think of how you'd answer the following questions:

- What have you done instead when you didn't want to use or drink?

- What have you said to yourself when you chose to abstain?

- What have you done to keep from missing the drugs or alcohol?

- With whom have you chosen to spend time when you were avoiding drugs or alcohol?

- Where have you gone to avoid drugs or alcohol?

- What kinds of things did you do with your diet, hygiene, sleep habits, or exercise to help you not drink or use?

- How have you talked yourself out of accepting high-risk opportunities? How did you decline them?

- Who have you relied on for help when you didn't want to use or drink?

- How have you praised yourself for not using or drinking when you chose to abstain?

- Have you been glad when certain people have been happy with your decisions to not indulge?

- Have you felt a sense of accomplishment or pride when you've chosen to not use?

- What else have you felt capable of when you have chosen to not use or drink?

Write down your low-risk thoughts, attitudes, and behaviors on your second list. Be as thorough as you were with your first list. Give names, addresses, dates, and specific examples. One-word answers don't count. Give details. Your work on these two lists will help you begin your actual lifestyle change and recovery, beginning with the sixth goal of this process. You want to make sure your work on this goal is as good as you can get it. A good way to make sure you're being as thorough and honest as possible is to go over the list with one of your sources of support. There will be more suggestions on how to go about this in the next section.

## Examining Your Lifestyle—Low-Risk Thoughts, Attitudes, and Behaviors

Write five thoughts, five attitudes, and ten behaviors you have used to help you those times when you have chosen to not use drugs or drink. Again, if you cannot think of ten right away, just write however many you can name.

1. _____

2. _____

3. _____

4. _____

5. _____

6. _____

7. _____

8. _____

9. _____

10. _____

11. _____

12. _____

13. _____

14. _____

15. _____

16. _____

17. _____

18. _____

19. _____

20. _____

# Admitting Your Lifestyle Characteristics

In order to make sure that your lists are thorough, accurate and fair to yourself, you need to discuss them with someone. This is similar to the concept in the fifth step of AA: "Admitted to God, to ourselves and to another human being the exact nature of our wrongs." The key concept from the fifth step, *admitted,* means "acknowledge." With this recovery process, make sure your lists of lifestyle characteristics are complete by *discussing* and *acknowledging* your lists with whatever source of support can help you do this the most.

Christopher was a young man in a group I led. He had told the group about four devastating years of drug addiction that bothered everyone who heard it. When he presented to the group his list of high-risk thoughts, attitudes, and behaviors, the group was stunned by what he *didn't* include. Christopher didn't include any mention of his drug suppliers or gang members who, in earlier group sessions, he'd already indicated were high-risk people for him. He hadn't mentioned that visiting his brother was a high-risk behavior because the part of town where his brother lived was a haven for drug suppliers. He didn't mention the fact that when he had more than twenty dollars on him at one time he would almost certainly score drugs because of an attitude that, when he had ready cash, he was invincible. He didn't write down that feeling bored was a high-risk attitude for him, and always led him to contact a high-risk person to find something to do.

Christopher became angry when confronted with these omissions. He kept insisting that because he'd spent three days working on his list, he'd done enough on it already and should be allowed to move on. With kind but firm persistence, the group whittled away his resistance. Christopher returned the next day with a revised list that was more realistic and thorough.

Megan, another patient in different circumstances, had a list of low-risk thoughts, attitudes, and behaviors that was more of a problem than her list of high-risk characteristics. Megan listed many complicated or unusual things that, while certainly low risk, were not the things a solid recovery plan were made of. She included behaviors which promoted her abstinence such as "skydiving, singing 'The Messiah,' and visiting archeological digs in

Africa." For low-risk attitudes she included "feeling like an eleven on a scale of one to ten." For a low-risk thought she included "not thinking I should be more mature than I am." Her source of support that helped her review her list pointed out that these events were either rare occurrences in her life, or were very difficult to define. Surely she wouldn't go skydiving often enough to make it a regular recovery activity. And how could any source of support objectively help her figure out if she was an eleven, as opposed to an eight and-a-half or a nine?

Megan agreed that some of her listed characteristics were too private to be things that could actually help her recovery. She completely changed all of those characteristics listed above except one. She realized she liked singing more than just "The Messiah" once a year, and decided to revise that one to simply "singing in front of people."

Hayden, on the other hand, used the opportunity to list his high-risk characteristics as an opportunity to criticize himself harshly. He gave examples, but peppered each one with a nasty judgment. An example included "When I have a screw-it-all attitude, I'll probably use again because I'm a selfish person who would rather hurt other people than be a decent human being." In session we discussed how difficult it was to read this and apply it toward his recovery. Did Hayden need to work on his attitude? Did he want to work on his selfishness? Did that statement really help his recovery?

We talked about the tone of Hayden's list. He was troubled by his memories of what he had done while active in his addiction. He was hoping to address those feelings immediately. Eventually, he agreed to wait on that, and focus now on learning how to maintain abstinence. Hayden said he understood that his feelings would not go away soon, that if he waited a month or so to address them, they wouldn't be any worse than they were right then. He agreed to rewrite his list of high-risk characteristics to put the focus on what he had done, not what he was feeling about having done it. In the end, he was more successful at recovery than he probably otherwise would have been.

You should acknowledge to at least one human (and living) source of support the exact nature of your high-risk and low-risk thoughts, attitudes, and behaviors. This is important if you want the rest of this process to work for you to help you stay abstinent.

As mentioned throughout this book, you don't have to make this therapeutic process spiritual. If, however, you find comfort in praying or discussing your lifestyle characteristics with a god, then do that. But to get the best results from this goal, you need a person to help you check your work. Make sure you're identifying the lifestyle characteristics as thoroughly as possible, by thinking of your first lists as rough drafts. Discussing them with someone will help you be more complete because you'll be forced to acknowledge things that you may be trying to quickly brush over, but in fact may be points you need to examine more closely. You need an objective perspective. (You may even find that more than one source of support gives you more effective feedback.)

For example, you may be tempted to excuse your high-risk characteristics by blaming your use of drugs or alcohol on someone else. Your source of support can point this out to you and help you focus on the real problem, namely, *your* behavior.

It's very possible that you want to claim that all your high-risk thoughts, attitudes, and behaviors are someone else's fault. You might have made a list of the ways others irritate you rather than a list of your own characteristics. You might even say you don't have any high-risk characteristics, or that you don't really care about them, so they're not really high-risk. Your source of support can help you avoid all those pitfalls. It's important for your recovery.

On the other hand, your source of support can also keep you from being too hard on yourself. Without meaning to, you might exaggerate your characteristics, or condemn yourself too harshly. You might end up making a list that doesn't give you any credit at all for your healthy, low-risk characteristics. Maybe you've forgotten some of the ways you have abstained or even relapsed. Your source of support can help you by talking about your past with you, asking probing questions, and stirring your memories up in general so that your lists are more helpful to you. Answering these questions, and others, will allow you to solidify your examples and give you a firmer understanding of what exactly you need to change in your life to become healthier.

Then, if in the course of the discussion, you realize that you need to add something to either one of your lists, you can do so. Take away anything that shouldn't be on the lists too. Strengthening your lists will improve your ability to succeed at recovery and remain abstinent in the long run. Your source of support may tell you to do this also.

Remember, the first set of lists are your rough drafts—you will need to revise them no matter how good you think you made them in the first place. Don't despair! The more work you put into this recovery goal now, the more likely you'll maintain your abstinence later. What may seem like a short-term hassle will have long-term benefits.

You should expect that your trusted source of support will question and challenge you. The questioning should never belittle you, but help you make your lists honest, strong, and useful. You can count on having to explain yourself.

This goal contains a lot of work and responsibility for you. Again, remember that the more work you put into it, the more strength your recovery will have. The work in this goal will be the foundation for your lifestyle change in the next goals of this process.

# Reaching Your Fourth Goal

With this fourth goal, you examine both your lifestyle and the things you do that help you relapse or abstain. To complete this examination, you discuss your lifestyle characteristics with at least one of your sources of support. Here is the therapeutic statement for your fourth goal:

> *I make a thorough list of those thoughts, attitudes, and behaviors I use to set myself up to relapse, and another list of those thoughts, attitudes, and behaviors I use to keep myself abstinent; then I share and revise my lists with at least one of my sources of support.*

Once you know these things about yourself, you can change your lifestyle for the better. However, do you feel ready to make those changes? The next goal will help you answer that question and prepare to make the changes.

# 5

## Make a Commitment to Change

You have completed a lot of work, thus far, with this process. Before you go on, you should make sure you feel ready to commit to a permanent lifestyle change. This goal will help you make that commitment and become ready to make those changes.

The basis for this goal comes from the sixth and seventh steps of AA. As they were originally written, these two steps reflect Bill Wilson's spiritual nature more than any of the others. Bill believed that at this point, AA members would need to work on improving their personal relationships, which would improve their relationship with God. This is how Bill believed AA members would stay sober. With the therapeutic process, however, this fifth goal will help you get ready for changes to help you stay abstinent, but you won't stay abstinent by improving your relationships. Instead, you'll make changes more directly relating to your use of drugs and alcohol. It's almost like changing your relationship with drugs and alcohol instead of your personal ones.

The sixth and seventh steps of AA read: "Were entirely ready to have God remove all these defects of character," and "Humbly

asked Him to remove our shortcomings." In this goal, you'll focus on the following key terms from the AA steps: "defects of
character," "shortcomings," "God," "Him," "entirely ready," and
"humbly."

## A Reminder about "God" and "Him"

Here, as in the second and fourth goals, you should remember that for the purposes of the therapeutic goals, you work with
sources of support. While these may include God, you have no requirement to include God. Include whoever and whatever you
need to help you get and maintain abstinence. This concept only
refers to your sources of support.

## "Defects of Character" and "Shortcomings"

These terms give these steps the same moral undertone that
the fourth step had. Again, the concept that's important to this
process is knowing the difference between right and wrong. Because this is a chemical dependency recovery process, the idea becomes knowing the difference between how to stay abstinent and
how to relapse.

If you want to recover from drug or alcohol dependency, you
must get rid of those parts of your lifestyle allowing you to use or
drink. Furthermore, you must strengthen those lifestyle characteristics keeping you abstinent. When you make a commitment to
change, you complete this goal. Your work on the rest of the goals
in this recovery process rely on that commitment. You can develop the ability to avoid relapse and stay abstinent; however,
you'll succeed at this only if you commit completely to change.

## "Entirely Ready" and "Humbly"

Consider the term *entirely ready* from the sixth step. When
you feel entirely ready, you feel completely prepared; you're
ready to take action *now*. To succeed in recovery, you must commit completely to take action without any reservations. You'll not

remain abstinent if you make a commitment to take only *some* of the action required. That simply won't work.

During the third goal, you committed to do some work. Now, with this fifth goal, you commit to change your life. Completely. You cannot achieve this on your own; if you could have, you would have done so before getting this book. To achieve the change, you must have the help of sources of support. Complete commitment means you feel ready and willing to accept the guidance and advice of your sources of support.

After this goal, you'll make plans to change living a lifestyle that supports your chemical dependency to one supporting your recovery. This is hard, and you should not attempt it on your own; it simply won't work that way. Chemical dependency is a powerful thing. It affects your body, your mind, and your emotions. That doesn't leave you with much that's unaffected to begin or maintain your recovery. Allow yourself the courage to seek the help of people who know more about abstinence than you know right now. It won't be a sign of weakness, it will be a sign of healthy humbleness.

Humbleness is one of the concepts of the seventh step. The word *humbly*, from the adjective *humble*, means, "modest or unpretentious in character ... devoid of pride or arrogance." At this point in your recovery, you need to be humble. That means you have to admit that right now, your own best efforts don't work well enough to keep you abstinent. You need the advice and guidance of sources of support in order to recover from chemical dependency. Recovery will occur only when you rely on the help of people and things that have more ability to help you get abstinent and avoid relapse than you have on your own.

The following two examples will show how important this concept is. A patient of mine, Michael, said he came from a culture where men did not ask for help. Men were supposed to be in charge of their lives, and only weak men "bared their souls" to anyone else. He had been attending support groups, but refused to speak to anyone there, usually arriving late and leaving early. A few of his friends at work offered to help him, but he thanked them without a commitment. Two men also from his culture even suggested he let them help him privately, but he declined.

When Michael began to work on this goal, he decided to stop attending treatment. He said treatment wasn't helping him anyway, so he didn't see why he should continue. In reality, Michael wasn't understanding some of the things people said at the support groups he attended. However, since he never spoke to anyone there, he never gave himself the chance to get clear. Michael based his ability to maintain abstinence on a personal belief that he could overcome anything with determination and, if necessary, an intimidating display of anger. Michael maintained abstinence for four weeks before he began drinking again. Many of his peers and family saw it coming—he began to withdraw from others, and more importantly, he became increasingly angry when anyone asked how his recovery was doing. The straw that broke the camel's back was when his wife innocently asked him if he'd ever gotten a sponsor. He flew into a rage, went to a bar, and continued to rage until he passed out drunk, just before the police arrived.

Cori, on the other hand, embraced the idea of humble commitment from the beginning. She had already failed at one effort to maintain abstinence on her own, and was kicked out of an earlier outpatient treatment program because of how she expressed her resistance. When she began residential treatment, she said she was getting good advice from family, friends, social workers, and a minister, but none of them were really familiar with addictions or recovery. She wanted to get it right this time, which to her meant taking the advice of therapists and people who had "sober time" in the support groups she attended. She frequently asked for help, clarification, and suggestions. In fact, some of her peers in treatment said they wished they could be more like Cori, since she seemed to be more willing to succeed in treatment than they were. Cori finished her treatment faster than anyone else who started at the same time she did, and continues to be a role model for other people in recovery.

Don't allow your pride to get in the way. Let go of any resistance which could keep you from making changes. Without that humbleness, you will not hold on to abstinence. Without humbleness, you will not maintain your recovery.

# Discussing Your Commitment to Change with a Source of Support

No worksheet alone can help you achieve this goal. You should consider this responsibility carefully and discuss it with at least one of your sources of support. Your remaining goals will help you make permanent lifestyle changes. Are you ready to do that? Are you ready to follow the advice of others to help you change your lifestyle? You'll recover only if you feel unreservedly and completely prepared to follow their advice. Of course, you'll not find this easy. Talk about this with some of your sources of support. The other possibility is that you might feel entirely ready *now* to do this. What if you realize that your changes need to include finding new ways to celebrate and socialize? Check that feeling against the following thoughts:

- Are you ready to reconsider how you'll celebrate the special days in your life and your friends' lives? Will you be willing to do things differently at the next bachelor or bachelorette party? How about the next baby or bridal shower? What about a birthday or anniversary? What about reunions? Should you discuss these things with someone to make sure you're ready to change in the best way for your recovery?

- Are you willing to change the ways you socialize? Are you willing to learn how to date without drugs or alcohol? How about having a girls' night out? Boys' night out?

- Are you willing to change the way you celebrate or socialize with your own particular culture or ethnic group? Can you participate at a religious service differently even if you've always expected to find alcohol or drugs available at those things? Are you ready to learn how to decline drinking or using with your elders or peers even if that goes against the grain of "your people"? Should you discuss this with someone, maybe someone from your culture, to make sure you're ready?

Are you ready to stop your chemical dependency for good? If you have any reservations, talk them over with your sources of support. Look over your self-diagnosis again. Review your lists from the fourth goal. Remember why you want to change?

Audrey was a patient who was unsure if she was really ready or not. She truly wanted to make her life better, but she was afraid she would be giving up too much if she gave up her drinking. Her lifestyle, social life, and reputation were based on drinking. She and I reviewed her first goal lists, and she became overwhelmed again by the damage her drinking had caused, despite all the good she thought it did for her. She knew whatever humbling discomfort she would go through in recovery would be nothing like the humiliation she had created for herself already.

Most of the people I've worked with are more like Jeffrey. Jeffrey, having completed the prior four goals, only needed one night to think about whether or not he was ready to change. He told me he was sure he wanted his life to get better, and he was willing to make big changes to do it. He told me he wanted to learn how to do it, because he wasn't exactly sure. He and I both knew he was ready.

As you think about all this, keep in mind the importance of following the guidance of your sources of support. Sometimes their advice may seem unwelcome and confining. If you feel that way, just remember: Many people know more about staying free from drugs and alcohol than you do, especially right now as you just get started. Even when it's inconvenient, you'll serve yourself best by following the advice of those sources of support.

**Ready?**

## *Reaching Your Fifth Goal*

This goal helps you commit yourself to the work you will do in the next five goals. After this one, your life will change in some wonderful and healthy ways—as long as you let it change that way. Talk this over until you feel prepared. When you feel ready, then you should go on to the next goal. Here is the goal statement for the fifth goal:

> *I feel entirely ready to humbly follow the guidance of my sources of support to help me reduce my relapse-prone behavior and improve my chances for abstinence.*

When you can make this statement, the time comes for planning your permanent changes. That begins with the next goal.

# 6

## Draft Your Plan
## of Action

Take a moment to recognize how much work you've already accomplished. You have diagnosed yourself with chemical dependency, identified sources of support to help you recover, made a commitment to work, examined your high-risk and low-risk lifestyle characteristics, and then made a stronger commitment to use the advice of your sources of support to change your lifestyle. This is a lot of good work, and to keep it up you've now got to begin planning those lifestyle changes.

With this goal you'll create a plan of action, a blueprint that will help you keep in charge of lifestyle changes and your recovery. You will not yet put the plan into effect. This plan of action will guide you while you change your lifestyle. You'll use the plan to help you develop lasting abstinence and avoid relapse.

This goal uses the concepts from the eighth step of Alcoholics Anonymous: "Made a list of all persons we had harmed, and became willing to make amends to them all." The eighth step helps an AA member begin to improve personal relationships as the way to maintain abstinence. As noted in chapter 5, in this

therapeutic process you don't recover by improving your relationships. You achieve recovery through other lifestyle changes. Still,
a few of the terms and concepts from the eighth step are worth re-
viewing.

## Another List

You've made five lists so far in this process. Time to make
two more. One list will help you plan ways to avoid relapse. The
other list will help you plan specific ways to remain abstinent.
These plans of action will help you restore sound judgment to
your life. As with your other lists, it will be important for you to
write them down so you can review your work and rely on your
plan for a long time to come.

## Make Amends

The word *amends* can mean "reparation." The plan you create
with this goal will help you make reparations; that is, you will
make some repairs. You will make repairs on the way you have
lived your life. These repairs are improvements and will help you
stay abstinent and avoid relapse.

The plan of action that you're going to draft will help you
change your unhealthy thoughts, attitudes, and behaviors. To
make this plan most effective, you need to focus on just yourself
and on your drug or alcohol use.

## All Persons We Had Harmed

Think about this task: What if you made a list of all the people you had harmed because of your drinking or use of drugs.
Now, what if you ranked that list, starting with the name of the
person you hurt the most at the top of the list. Who's name would
be at the top of your list? Your answer to that question should be,
"Myself."

Certainly, you may have done awful things to other people.
Nevertheless, you would have always felt your own personal
shame, guilt, and remorse more intensely. Others react to what
you do, but they can always leave you or avoid you. You have to
live with yourself. You have to relive those awful things in your
mind, over and over. Even if your actions have been so awful that

you have killed someone, you have continued to live, and you have lived with the fact that you took that person's life. That's quite a burden to have forced yourself to endure.

You have harmed yourself the most because of your dependency. That is why you should make a plan only to change your own life. Do not try to figure out how you might get others to change. Developing a plan of action for yourself will, in the long run, actually do more for everyone in your life if you help yourself first.

# Don't Plan Too Much Too Soon

As has been mentioned several times in this book, right now your plan of action should only deal with overcoming your chemical dependency. That's enough work for you for now! As you think about these significant lifestyle changes, you should avoid trying to make almost any other changes in your life.

Alcoholics Anonymous and Narcotics Anonymous each have an unwritten tradition recommending that members should avoid major life decisions in the first year of recovery. This is good advice. At this early point in your recovery you shouldn't begin a brand new love relationship, start the ball rolling to make a major purchase, change jobs, adopt a child, change religions, or make other big decisions. You should wait for some time before deciding to do any of these things. You may not need to wait an entire year, but don't start them now. You might consider such important decisions when you work on goals eight or nine in this process, but not now.

## *The Exceptions*

Of course, if making this kind of an important decision would definitely help you stay abstinent, then make it. For example, if your job always leads you to use or drink, because you can't resist the opportunities to drink or use when you work, for example, as a bartender or in a pharmacy, then you should change jobs. In that case, that kind of major life decision would help you protect your abstinence. If being an officer at a civic organization always means you drink with the membership, then you should resign your position. If you do, you will be helping yourself avoid relapse.

Go ahead and make big changes if you really must do them for practical reasons. Just because you have recently begun recovery doesn't necessarily mean you should cancel your wedding, turn down a promotion, or back out of a legal transaction. However, if doing any of these would definitely lead you to relapse, then by all means, don't do them.

Also, if you're in a dangerous situation and must take some action to get you out of danger, then take that action. For example, if you owe more money than you can pay a loan shark, maybe you should go to the police or move away. Or, if you live in an abusive home or are in a relationship with someone who abuses you, then you might need to take some action. Perhaps you should leave the situation for a healthier place somewhere else. This could be temporary, it could be permanent. Once you're safe, get back to work on your recovery.

The best way for you to make these kinds of decisions is with the help of a source of support. At this point in the process, you're still just learning how to maintain abstinence. Your recovery is fragile. Trying to make a major change like this will be a high risk thing for you to do. Don't do it alone. Ask a source, or several sources of support for their help, advice, guidance, and support. Plan strategies with them on how you can make these kinds of decisions but still maintain your abstinence. Should you check in with a source of support frequently? Can you let a support group know what you're doing, then give updates at each meeting? Should you have someone actually help you while you make the change?

These are all ways that your sources of support can help you when you need to make major life decisions early in your recovery. You can make those decisions and still maintain your abstinence. Do that, and continue with this process as much as you can while doing that. For now, you were just getting ready to start making your plan of action.

# Making Your Plan of Action

The plan of action you're going to create has two parts. One part will help you avoid high-risk characteristics that make you prone to relapse, like the ones you identified in chapter four. The other part will help you strengthen and increase the frequency of your low-risk characteristics that help you maintain abstinence. The first part then, helps you avoid relapse; the second part helps you maintain abstinence. Together, these two parts form one impressive plan that will help you recover.

This goal just helps you make the plan, then get ready to put it into action. With the next goal, you'll actually put the plan into action. This is the way you'll continue your recovery from now on—day by day. After this one, the following goals will each help you learn more ways to figure out how to avoid relapse and maintain your abstinence. Over the weeks and months, your plan will need to evolve, bit by bit. The longer you continue recovery, the more you will need to make slight changes in your plan of action. In a year, the plan you develop now will seem simple compared to what you're going to do with it.

The work you do for this goal is basically the work you'll do forever to keep yourself abstinent, free from relapse, and in recovery. For right now, however, you're going to spend a few days developing your first plan of action to avoid relapse and maintain abstinence.

Make a plan of action which helps you avoid your high-risk thoughts, attitudes, and behaviors, and which helps you generate more of your low-risk thoughts, attitudes, and behaviors. In other words, create a plan which can help you avoid relapse and maintain abstinence. You might wonder how you're going to figure out what you should put into your plan. Where will you get ideas? Remember those lists you wrote for goal four? Time to check them out again.

The two lists from your fourth goal will help you understand what in your life needs to change. On those lists you wrote twenty low- and high-risk thoughts, attitudes, and behaviors. Based on the information you have on those lists, you'll write your plan to avoid relapse and stay abstinent. You can begin your work on this sixth goal quickly. Be sure to fine-tune your plan before considering yourself finished and moving on.

Make sure you write down or somehow record this plan. Write on paper, use your journal, dictate to someone else, use a tape recorder, or write in this book. During stressful times, you can refer back to your plan. You could think of this plan as another source of support. Or, you can use the plan to remind you of the actions you decided would help you stay abstinent. It will also help you remember those things you shouldn't do that could set you up for relapse.

## Planning Yourself Out of Your High-Risk Characteristics

Think about what things you'll put on your plan to deal with your high-risk thoughts, attitudes, and behaviors. Be sure to include many details. Your plan should address everything that you put on your list of high-risk characteristics. The following scenarios will hopefully give you some ideas on how to structure your plan.

### High-Risk Behaviors

You might be tempted to just write the words "I will never" thirty times, and then copy whatever was on your list of high-risk characteristics. That's not a plan of action, that's just a list of promises. You should do more than that.

For example, say you wrote on your list for goal four that "Spending time with Stacy usually ends up with me using drugs because Stacy encourages me to use and hassles me if I refuse." Now, your plan of action needs to be more than just "I won't spend time with Stacy." This is too general and really won't help you know what to do when the situation arises. You need steps to take or rules to follow that will guide you away from falling into old, dangerous patterns.

Think of what would be part of a better plan. How will you avoid Stacy? What if you bump into Stacy unexpectedly? What if Stacy calls? What if Stacy is a relative you live with? A better plan of action in this case would be this:

- I won't contact Stacy.

- I won't return Stacy's calls.

- I won't go to Max's house, because I know Stacy usually hangs out there.

- If I do run into Stacy, I will say that I'm not into drugs anymore and won't be spending time with people who use anymore.

- I'll let Pat and Tracy know that Stacy is bad news for me.

- If Stacy won't leave me alone, I'll seek out Pat or Tracy and ask them to help me avoid Stacy.

Now that's a plan. The plan is detailed enough to be effective and take care of this situation. However, the steps are broad enough to also help you if someone else becomes a high-risk person in your life; you could deal with that person in much the same way you deal with Stacy. So, you can use this part of your plan even beyond this one situation.

### High-Risk Attitudes

How would you develop a plan to handle a high-risk attitude? If you put "When I feel left out because I can't drink, I'll often go drown my sorrows" on your high-risk attitude list, you need a strong plan to deal with that. You can probably see that "Don't feel left out" would be a pretty useless plan of action.

How will you avoid a high-risk attitude? Who will you talk with about it? What will you do to improve your attitude?

Here's an example of a good plan:

- I will exercise at least three times each week to help me keep my spirits up.

- I will ask my supervisor to help me understand certain areas of my job better so I won't get mad at the work I do.

- I will talk with other people at my support group meeting to try to understand how they cope with feeling left out and having a high-risk attitude.

- If I start to get jealous over someone or some situation where I feel left out, I will leave the situation and go talk with a calmer person about the problem before I get too down.

- Every day I will think about how long I've stayed alcohol-free, and let myself feel proud of that achievement.

There's enough detail in this plan so that it should work for you under a lot of different situations. A few weeks from now, if you discovered that you had another problem attitude like "recovery isn't worth the hassle," this plan would be just as effective for you to deal with that.

**High-Risk Thoughts**

What kind of plan of action will help you overcome high-risk thoughts? Again, you need to include detail in your plan. Suppose you wrote this high-risk thought on your list: "Wondering if I could use or drink again if I used or drank only a little bit leads me to relapse." This is a high-risk thought a lot of chemically dependent people have.

How do you plan to deal with it? Having a plan saying "I'll never want to use again," isn't realistic; it's too weak a plan to help you out. You'll be surprised at how often you might think this kind of high-risk thought. Here's a better plan:

- Every day I'll look at the list that I made of high-risk thoughts, attitudes, and behaviors from the fourth goal.

- I'll think of how many of the problems on my list happened when I was trying to control my drinking or drug use.

- I'll think about my former friends who are still trying to control their use, remembering that none of them are successful at it.

- I'll stop wondering if I could still drink or use "just a little bit" based on my conclusions of these examinations.

- I'll call my friend Jamie to talk me out of it if I ever do have the high-risk thought that I can have just a little.

Once again, this kind of planning could help you with more thoughts than just this one, which is what you want to achieve by making this whole plan of action.

## Strengthen Your Low-Risk Characteristics

Think about the things that you will put on your plan of action to improve, increase, and strengthen your low-risk thoughts, attitudes, and behaviors. Again, these things need to be specific to help you with each item you identified in your low-risk list from the fourth goal, while also being general enough to help you make big lifestyle changes. You might feel tempted again to just rewrite your fourth goal list of low-risk thoughts, attitudes, and behaviors. This, however, is not a good idea. Instead, use what you said to help you make a plan. Consider the following examples.

### Low-Risk Behaviors

Say you put "Spending time with the kids" on your list of abstinence-protecting behaviors from your fourth goal. How will you create a plan to do this? Make some specific plans and promises; "I will spend time with the kids" is simply not detailed enough. Think about the following steps you can plan to take:

- I'll spend at least a half-hour every weekday with the kids talking with them or helping them with their homework.

- I'll make sure the TV won't be on during our half-hour.

- I'll make it a point to eat dinner with the kids at least four nights each week.

- We'll do something every weekend together, whether it's just taking them to the store with me, or going on a big trip to an amusement park, the beach, or a park.

- I'll choose to do something with them instead of using drugs or drinking.

Ah, now that's a plan. It's specific—you're giving yourself definite tasks to accomplish. It's also broad—you can give yourself credit for having an alternative to using or drinking by just taking the kids with you to the hardware store. Good job.

### Low-Risk Attitudes

Consider how you'll improve your attitude with this plan. Again, you need details. If you wrote that "Feeling proud of my job performance" is an attitude helping you stay abstinent, develop a plan making sure this happens. You need something more useful than "I will feel proud of having a job." Here's an example of a detailed, helpful plan to increase your low-risk attitudes:

- I will try to improve my productivity at work.

- I will volunteer for some new assignment at work.

- I will ask for frequent performance evaluations during my first year in recovery.

- I will try to make my performance ratings better between each evaluation.

- I will remember, every day, that my performance was never this good when I was using or drinking

- I will remind myself that my performance is as good as it is now because I'm abstinent.

This plan will help you stay abstinent. And if you do it long enough, this plan will probably help you advance at your job, or even get you a better job. This is another example of a good and broad plan of action.

## Low-Risk Thoughts

Now, think of how you'll plan to change your thoughts to improve your low-risk characteristics. If put on your fourth goal list "Drugs and alcohol cost me too much," then what can you do to remind yourself of that thought and improve your chances to stay abstinent? Consider the following plan for perpetuating that low-risk thought:

- I will not spend money on drugs or alcohol.

- I'll figure out how much money I have NOT spent on drugs or alcohol every week.

- I'll look at my credit-card statements and my bank statements every month to see how things have improved since I stopped spending money on drugs or alcohol.

- I will budget the money I used for drugs or alcohol to pay off my debts within eighteen months.

- I will invest in certificates of deposit or in a retirement fund at least half the money I was spending every month on drugs or alcohol.

With this plan, you'll motivate yourself to not spend money on your chemical dependency. You'll also start to save; good plan! Do you think you understand how to do this? Well, then it's time to do it.

# Draft Your Plan of Action

Write your plan in this book or on a separate piece of paper, like a page in your journal. Your plan should look a lot like the previous examples. On the first page, write your relapse-prevention (to counteract your high-risk characteristics) plan. On the other, write an abstinence-protecting (to strengthen your low-risk characteristics) plan. While you work on these plans, think of how you would answer the following questions, which are similar to the ones you answered when you worked on the fourth goal.

## *Relapse-Prevention Plan*

Now that you've considered examples of a good plan and figured out both your high- and low-risk characteristics, you're ready to draft your plan. First, work on your plan to prevent relapse. Take every thought, attitude, and behavior you wrote on your fourth goal, high-risk list, and come up with a plan to avoid it. Answer these questions for every thought, attitude, and behavior:

- How can you avoid getting drugs or alcohol?

- Who should you avoid calling?

- Who should you avoid visiting?

- How will you avoid them?

- Where should you not go?

- What kinds of events should you avoid?

- What will you do to keep from going there?

- What should you do to avoid setting yourself up to use or to drink?

- What relapse-preventing things should you make it a point to do every day, every week, every month?

- What are the things you should avoid doing so that you won't trick yourself or someone else into getting drugs or alcohol?

- What kind of mind games that you play with yourself should you learn to recognize? How will you deal with those mind games?

- What are thoughts you should recognize that in the past have signaled an upcoming relapse?

- How should you deal with those thoughts?

- What else should you do to avoid relapse?

## A Plan Preventing Me from Relapse

Here's a plan of action that will help me avoid relapse. I will do these things to help me deal with high-risk thoughts, attitudes, and behaviors:

1. _____

2. _____

3. _____

4. _____

5. _____

6. _____

7. _____

8. _____

9. _____

10. _____

11. _____

12. _____

13. _____

14. _____

15. _____

16. _____

17. _____

18. _____

19. _____

20. _____

## Protecting Abstinence

Now it's time to work on part two—protecting your abstinence with your low-risk characteristics. What things should you include for this part of your plan of action? How will you increase your chances to stay abstinent? This part of your plan on the low-risk thought, attitudes, and behaviors will come from the list you made on your fourth goal. Write these ideas down on a second page in your journal, or on another piece of paper. Ask yourself the following questions as you develop this plan:

- With whom should you spend more time?

- What should you do to fill your spare time?

- What hobbies or interests should you begin pursuing more?

- How will you make sure to pursue them?

- How should you let people know about your changes if they ask about them or invite you to a high-risk activity?

- How should you make it known that you're now abstaining from drugs and alcohol?

- How can you keep a positive attitude about your abstinence? What should you do to make it seem worthwhile?

- Will your pride increase as you feel you're spending more and more time not drinking or using drugs?

- Is the opinion of anyone in particular important to you?

- How will you talk to those people about your abstinence?

- How can you reward yourself for staying abstinent?

- Will spending some time thinking about your success in recovery help?

- What should you look for to recognize the benefits from staying abstinent?

## A Plan Protecting My Abstinence

Here is a plan of action that will help me maintain my abstinence. I will do these things to strengthen low-risk thoughts, attitudes, and behaviors:

1. _____
2. _____
3. _____
4. _____
5. _____
6. _____
7. _____
8. _____
9. _____
10. _____
11. _____
12. _____
13. _____
14. _____
15. _____
16. _____
17. _____
18. _____
19. _____
20. _____

## Get Some Input

During your work on this goal, don't forget to get some feedback and guidance from your sources of support. Take your plan that you've drafted to a support group or to a certain individual for input. You should include someone else in your process of recovery. Like you did with the fourth goal, discuss your plan of action with at least one source of support in order to help make your plan solid. Talk with this person also to help you become ready to put your plan to work.

# Become Willing

When you make this plan of action, you prepare to make lifestyle changes. These changes are serious, they last forever. They represent even more commitment on your part. No matter how long or how short it takes you to come up with both parts of your plan of action, you'll probably need a little more time to get ready to put the plan into effect. Spend some time now to work on becoming willing to put your plan into effect.

Let's look at the word *willing* from the eighth step: When the Twelve Steps were written the word was defined as "disposed or consenting (without being particularly desirous . . .)." See how the term could apply here? You should *become ready* to act on your plan, even if you don't feel particularly cheerful or desirous about doing so. You may not like it in the short run, but you'll stay abstinent and avoid relapse in the long run. You'll like that.

Take your plan of action to one source of support you particularly trust. Discuss your plan with him or her. Is it realistic? Should you make any parts more specific? Should you broaden anything in it? Should you discuss it with anyone else to make sure of its success? What else should you do to get ready to put the plan into effect?

One person I worked with as part of a group, Tyler, is a good example of becoming willing to put a plan of action into effect. Tyler had mentioned that visiting his girlfriend's house was a high-risk behavior for him. However, he had named his girlfriend as one of his sources of support. While she didn't use drugs, her brothers who lived in her house did. Over the last year, Tyler had developed a habit when he went to her house of spending as much time with her brothers using drugs as he did with his girlfriend (and this was one of his examples of unmanageability). The girlfriend wasn't financially able to move out of the house, her brothers were unwilling to discontinue their drug use, and her parents were unwilling to force the issue on them. Tyler developed a decent enough plan that dealt with all his other high-risk thoughts, attitudes, and behaviors; but this issue was a glaring omission on his plan.

When confronted, Tyler complained that by not going to his girlfriend's house, he was jeopardizing the relationship. Why should he be penalized, he complained, when it was his girlfriend's brothers' fault that the home was high risk? The group at first spoke with, then debated with Tyler over his points. What was more important, they asked, his recovery or his relationship? After all, would the relationship last if his recovery didn't? Tyler admitted that he couldn't avoid her brothers if he went to his girlfriend's house, and that he'd lose the relationship if he used drugs again. Still, he angrily insisted it was unfair, unreasonable, and unnecessary to require him to stop seeing his girlfriend.

This raised a red flag for several members of the group. They pointed out that the issue wasn't whether or not Tyler could never see his girlfriend again, the issue was that he shouldn't go to her house. When pushed, Tyler reported he'd never discussed this part of his recovery plan with his girlfriend. He was worried that she wouldn't understand how influential her brothers were to his addiction. He was also worried that in trying to explain it to her, she would become offended on behalf of her family at what he was suggesting. He didn't want to avoid her house without her support, and he was afraid to ask for it.

Everyone, including Tyler, had to admit that continuing to see his girlfriend might be an issue Tyler would need to evaluate sometime soon. For now though, Tyler wanted to do all he could to continue having her be a part of his life. He agreed to role-play some ways that he could bring the issue up with his girlfriend. After several practice tries, he said he was ready to add to his plan of action "avoid meeting my girlfriend at her house because of the influence of her brothers." He made a commitment to the group that he'd talk the matter over with his girlfriend within two days, and seek her input on improving this part of his plan with options for where the two of them could meet besides her house. And if he did need to pick her up at her house, she could help him by being ready to leave right when Tyler arrived to pick her up, and the two of them should not include her brothers in plans to go out. Two days later, at the next group session, everyone was delighted to hear that the conversation went great, his girlfriend was willing to have Tyler spend less time at her house while still seeing him, and that Tyler was able to strengthen his plan accordingly.

After some discussion with your sources of support, you will become ready to put your plan into action. It shouldn't take too long for you to become willing to follow through with your plan. You've probably already experienced some satisfaction with the amount of control you're feeling in your life now. When you put your plan to work, you'll feel even better.

## Reaching Your Sixth Goal

With this goal you make a plan of action that will help you prevent relapse and increase your chances to stay abstinent. Create a plan that changes your lifestyle so you won't have the opportunity to use or drink again. Create a plan boosting your ability to stay abstinent. Here is the therapeutic statement of your sixth goal:

> *I write a plan of action to prevent relapse and protect my abstinence, and prepare to put the plan into action.*

As you discuss this plan with others, you'll probably revise it. When you think you have revised it enough and are prepared and willing (that is, once you're ready to stick to the plan you created), then act on your plan. Carry it out. That's the work of your next goal.

# 7

## Put Your Plan to Work

Time now to put your plan to work and see how effective it is in helping you strengthen your ability to stay abstinent and avoid relapse. By putting your plan to work, you truly take charge of your new lifestyle and your recovery. By doing the work on this goal, you will answer these questions:

Does your plan work for you? And, do you have more on your plan than you should?

The ninth step of AA reads, "Made direct amends to such people wherever possible, except when to do so would injure them or others." Let's look at the important concepts in this step.

### "Made Amends"

With the ninth step, the AA member puts into action what was planned in the eighth step. The concept behind the word *made* means that now you will enact what you just finished planning in the previous chapter. Your plan of action is a way for you to make improvements in your life. Making improvements is, in turn, the concept behind the word *amends*. Amends make things better; so does your plan. With this goal you're going to start to make things better by putting your plan to work.

Of course, throughout your goal work you should have stayed abstinent. Now, however, you take more responsibility for your abstinence. Now you bring about changes in your lifestyle so that you can remain abstinent throughout your day-to-day living.

## *"Wherever Possible"*

Think of this concept in this way: You should practice your plan of action wherever possible. Recovery is not an isolated event. It is a process. Recovery gets stronger the longer you practice it. The need to practice your recovery program will never pass away. Your lifestyle changes are permanent. You must practice recovery wherever possible. Your plan of action affects every part of your life; don't think of your plan as just an occasional thing to do when it seems convenient.

Whether you find your abstinence fun and easy or tough and involved, you must consider your abstinence your first order of business. Practice your plan wherever possible, not just whenever you want.

## *"Except When to Do So Would Injure Them or Others"*

Once again, the focus of your recovery is yourself. Therefore, the concept from this step will also focus on you. There is one condition when you should not make your lifestyle changes the way you planned them. The ninth step tells AA members to avoid doing any emotional damage in the name of recovery by warning, "except when to do so would injure them or others." The process of recovery in this book should help you to recover in a healthy, satisfying way. You don't want to hurt anyone by maintaining your abstinence. In particular, you don't want to hurt yourself.

You may find some situations in your own recovery plan where, if you carried out your plan, you could actually hurt yourself or lead yourself to relapse. In these situations, you shouldn't continue with that part of your plan. Your recovery should never hurt you.

My patient Daniel's efforts are a good example of this. Daniel's addiction was to cocaine. He had first used when his two older brothers offered it to him in his late teens. While his brothers managed to cover most of their consequences, Daniel's use created more and more trouble for him. Seven years after he started, his life was a mess and he sought recovery. When making his plan, Daniel said that it would help his recovery if he confronted his brothers with their use of cocaine. Daniel and his brothers still lived at home, and Daniel thought it would be best to do this in front of their parents. Daniel assumed telling his parents about his and his brothers' drug use would force his brothers into recovery, create a better environment in his home, and bring his family closer together.

All of Daniel's support advised against this. No one thought it would help Daniel's recovery. After all, he didn't need his parents' approval or his brothers to get clean in order to maintain his own abstinence. There were options to dealing with his brothers' drug use that would be better for Daniel. Daniel listened to this feedback only half-heartedly.

Without telling any of his sources of support, Daniel confronted his brothers, in front of his parents over dinner. The result was a tremendous family argument that brought the neighbors over to try and calm things down. In the end, Daniel and his brothers were ordered out of the house, Daniel's mother refused to talk to any of them, his father threatened to call the police on the first son who tried to contact them, and Daniel's brothers swore out a vengeance on him that truly frightened him. Daniel, thinking he was only going to help carry out his plan of action, was now homeless, estranged from his family, and in danger.

Daniel discussed the fiasco with his sources of support. They chided him for choosing to ignore their advice. What was the point of calling them sources of support, they asked him, if he wasn't going to take their advice. Daniel agreed to listen more carefully to the advice his supports gave him. He continued with his plan of recovery. His desire to improve family matters, however, was put on hold for a while.

This recovery program focuses on your thoughts, attitudes, and behaviors. In any situation you face, you will always react with one of these three. When your reaction would make you likely to use or drink, then you should avoid the situation and change your reactions. Know that losing your abstinence will always be a greater hurt to you than whatever help you think the reaction might bring. Consider some examples.

### Focus on Yourself: Forget Convincing the Skeptics in Your Life

Some people will not believe your honesty or sincerity when you try to discuss your dependency with them. They won't trust that your efforts at recovery or your new lifestyle changes are for real. The low-risk decision will be for you to avoid those kinds of people for now. No amount of honesty or work on your part will make them more sensitive to your personal improvements.

These kinds of people include drug or alcohol suppliers, former using or drinking friends, chemically dependent family members who still drink or use, and people who can use or drink without being dependent (like "social drinkers" or people who very rarely use drugs, and always do so without consequence). If these people don't believe you have changed, then avoid them for now. They can't help your recovery anyway. If you push them too hard to believe you, they'll push back, and you'll be hurt. That sets you up for relapse.

### Focus on Yourself: Beware the Attitudes of People You Used to Hang Around

You will find that some of the people with whom you used to drink or use drugs will not like your newfound recovery. For a number of reasons, they might make things hard for you as you progress in recovery. Perhaps they are jealous of your improvements. Perhaps they feel threatened or betrayed by you. Perhaps they think you've become arrogant or pushy in your recovery. In any event, you may find that, like crabs that cling to each other as one is pulled out of a bucket, your former companions might try to pull you back down into a relapse. They might offer you drugs, sneak drugs into your home or your pockets, use or drink in front of you, or "dare" you to indulge again.

Keep your focus on yourself. You can't help these people now. Keep to your plan of action and stay a step ahead of their efforts to bring you down. Don't visit them, leave the situation if they show up; talk things over and get reassurances from your sources of support.

### Focus on Yourself: Avoid People in Your Life Who Are Angry at You

As another example, perhaps you would like a former spouse, lover, or romantic partner to know that you've changed your lifestyle. However, your former partner screamed at you the last time you were together, and told you that the police would be called if you ever came near again.

At this point in your recovery, you would make a high-risk decision if you chose to go near that person. It would probably hurt their feelings, or at the very least, ruin their day. More importantly, it would not help your recovery to do it. You might get so upset over your ex's reaction that you might consider drowning your disappointment by drinking or using drugs.

### Focus on Yourself: Avoid High-Risk Situations

Another example of action that could threaten your abstinence is simply setting yourself up to do something you know darned well is high risk. You might try to claim that your plan of action requires you to get into a high-risk situation.

Perhaps, for example, you identified your pal Terry as a high-risk person in your life. Now you go to a party, bump into Terry, and guess who needs a ride home? You might begin to argue with yourself about whether or not you should take Terry home. After all, you're not really obligated—you didn't arrive with Terry, and you haven't spent time with Terry since you began recovery. On the other hand, Terry lives on your way, and you wouldn't actually have to go *into* Terry's apartment . . .

Can you see how this kind of a mind game could threaten your recovery? Stick to your plan of action. If you know you shouldn't spend time alone with Terry, then don't spend time alone with Terry. Period.

### Focus on Yourself: Forget Convincing Others to Join You in Recovery

You may find it upsetting, if not impossible, to get other dependent people to start their own recovery. Suppose one of your best friends—Chris—drank or used drugs with you in your past. Suppose also that Chris used to complain about drugs or alcohol, and talked about how good it would be to stop. Maybe Chris even encouraged you when you first started out in recovery.

Now that your recovery has really begun, however, Chris no longer talks about quitting and doesn't want to listen to you talk about your success at quitting. A couple of times you suggested that maybe Chris would like to quit too. In response, Chris got really mad and defensive and accused you of trying to be "super counselor" to everybody.

You should avoid Chris, at least for now. Even if you had not thought you should put Chris on your high-risk list from your fourth goal, you should understand that this person will not help your recovery. Trying to win anyone over to your point of view will not help you stay abstinent. If you keep on trying, you will become angry, upset, and maybe hurt enough to think about using or drinking again.

### Focus on Yourself: Living with a Chemically Dependent Person

Here's something particularly difficult: You'll find that making the low-risk choice to avoid certain people is especially difficult if you identify someone you live with, particularly your spouse or partner, as a high-risk person in your life. If this person encourages you to drink or use, or tries to sabotage your efforts at abstinence, then you cannot consider them a low-risk influence in your life or your recovery. A high-risk marriage presents difficult choices that you must make based upon emotional, financial, spiritual, religious, social, and practical reasoning. You shouldn't make such a decision on your own. Discuss the situation with some of your sources of support.

Some lucky recovering people in this situation have found that once they began recovery, their spouses or partners soon began recovery themselves. Other recovering people just maintained their recovery plan and remained abstinent regardless of what their spouses or partners did. When their spouses continued to drink or use, other recovering people found that they could continue in the relationship by developing more and more support for their abstinence from outside of the marriage or partnership. In some cases a temporary separation helped to solve problems in the relationship. Still others found they needed to end the relationship because they couldn't stay abstinent otherwise.

In all these cases, the recovering people placed their recovery above all else. As painful as it may seem, this is a low-risk behavior because the action supports recovery and helps you to stay abstinent.

### Focus on Your Recovery

You may find that some of your old friends tease or even pester you into drinking or using drugs again. In this case, make a *low*-risk decision and avoid them. After all, hanging out with these people could most likely bring on nothing but high-risk behavior.

You may also feel lonely at first when you avoid your former friends or associates in order to maintain your abstinence. It's time to make some lifestyle changes, which means you need to pursue new situations, or some of the same situations in a new way. You might, for example, make it a point to always have a source of support with you if you need to be around former drug-using associates. Avoid any situation, however, if you feel you have to apologize to someone for trying to start a new way of living. In any situation, making an apology for trying to become healthy will probably hurt you more than it will help.

At this part of your recovery anyway, avoid situations where people try to persuade you to drink or use. You don't need this! The next three goals give you the opportunity to examine and address these types of circumstances further.

# Give Yourself Extra Support

In the first weeks and sometimes months after beginning your abstinence, you may feel overwhelmed. Your lifestyle changes feel new, unfamiliar. You try to do them, but you're not living by them yet. Newly recovering people often find abstaining from drugs or alcohol leads to some grief. You may experience this because you miss your old lifestyle. This is normal, even if your old lifestyle created tremendous problems for you.

You may feel confusion, uncertainty, and insecurity. You might even wonder if recovery is really worth all the work. After all, you may be thinking, you didn't feel so bad while you were using or drinking. The dependency caused problems, but at least you felt like you had more control than you do now. If you suffer withdrawal symptoms, then you will experience these feelings even more intensely.

These insecurities will last until you experience the changes as a natural part of your new lifestyle. Then, recovery will seem familiar, you'll feel more in control and secure. Meanwhile, your relapse-prevention and abstinence-support plan should include opportunities for you to discuss these insecurities and uncertainties with others who can understand how you feel. You might consider one-on-one counseling, and definitely consider support groups.

Many different support groups exist for people while recovering from chemical dependency. You could probably find something close to where you live. There is a list of the national offices for some chemical dependency recovery organizations in chapter 13. Use these groups as another source of support for you. You can use the opinions of the members of a group as another source of help and guidance. An individual member or two may give you more personal advice or feedback on your plan of abstinence or relapse-prevention.

As you attend support groups, don't expect to find them instantly helpful. You'll probably feel shy when you first attend. You may even find that you notice the unattractive qualities of certain members faster than you do their helpful qualities. Certain groups will have a better ability to help you than others. There are no guarantees that every single meeting of AA, NA, Women for Sobriety, Secular Options for Sobriety, Rational Recovery, or another group will work as well as possible. You will need to attend a few different meetings before you find one that really satisfies you.

Just remember why you or anyone attends these kind of support groups. You want to get ideas and support for improving your abstinence and avoiding relapse—always make this your first reason for attending. Find those people and the programs that can help you; leave the other ones alone.

# Benefits of Following Your Plan

After your first few days of recovery, you'll find you're feeling better, thinking clearer, because your withdrawal symptoms have reduced in their severity.

Over the course of the following weeks and months, as your ability to abstain becomes more and more solid, you'll feel a sense of confidence and ability. This, in turn, will help your self-esteem. Many of your current relationships will improve and new relationships will start out healthier. Your ability to perform the other duties in your life (like parenting, work, financial, and other obligations) will improve too. Have patience; you may not feel like the benefits come quickly enough. If you maintain your abstinence, however, they will come.

Incidentally, you have something more to look forward to. Over the years, your family, friends, and colleagues probably have heard dozens of promises from you to make things better. They won't believe your newer promises at first. They *will*, however, believe what they can see. You will prove to them that you are improving as you stay abstinent longer and longer. This may take a while, but it will happen. When it does, people will start to trust you again. Most recovering people find this both surprising and comforting. Many of your relationships will improve as your recovery improves over your first few months. It is one of the side effects of recovery.

# Reaching Your Seventh Goal

At this point, you have completed a milestone. Your efforts to become abstinent have become efforts to *maintain* abstinence. You are changing your lifestyle. Continue to work at it patiently and consistently. You'll eventually get the hang of it. Here's the therapeutic statement for your seventh goal:

> *I put my plan to work, except when to do so would hurt someone more than it would help me.*

After a while, you may find some unexpected challenges while you live by your plan of action. For example, perhaps you hadn't anticipated a difficult situation like an unexpected illness, a major change in a relationship, or sudden unemployment. Or perhaps you overlooked a situation that you didn't think of as being a problem, like dealing with certain critical friends or relatives. Or perhaps something that seemed small to you ended up a bigger problem, like receiving alcoholic wine at a church communion service.

As you continue in recovery, you'll need to deal with these unexpected situations. If the plan of action you developed proves inadequate to deal with these new situations, you need to improve your plan. That is the work of the next goal.

# 8

# Modify Your Plan

Now you have put your plan of action into effect and you have lived by it. After a while, probably within a couple of months, you'll probably notice that your plan may not continue to be helpful enough just as it is now. While your plan is usually enough to help you remain abstinent, you might have found that it was lacking in some ways. New problems or issues in your life may have cropped up challenging your abstinence more than you had expected. Perhaps it's time to make some changes in your plan to make it even stronger and more useful. This goal helps you make the kinds of changes that will put you even more firmly in charge of changing your lifestyle to help you maintain your abstinence.

Your work on this goal can begin now. More work will happen weeks or months from now, after you've had more success in staying abstinent but face a problem you didn't anticipate would come up.

This goal calls for you to evaluate your plan of action, and change it to make it stronger where you need to. If you discover new challenges in your life threatening your abstinence, this goal helps you adjust your plan to meet those challenges. The changes will help you handle any new problems successfully. There is another side to this goal, however. If your plan works well enough to help you maintain abstinence, then you deserve to give yourself praise for that.

This goal uses the therapeutic concepts from the tenth step of AA. That step reads, "Continued to take personal inventory and when we were wrong, promptly admitted it." Compared to the other steps, members working on this one rely more on work they already completed in their past steps. Several concepts from this step should be explored in order to understand this therapeutic goal.

## "Continued to Take Personal Inventory"

*Continue* means to keep on doing something. So, to keep on recovering, just keep on doing the work you have done up to now. Now, however, broaden your work. Similar to the fourth goal, in this eighth goal the term *personal inventory* is interpreted to refer to your plan of action. So, this goal reminds you to continue your plan of action. But as you continue to make lifestyle changes, you will have other challenges in your life that you may not have realized would need your attention (there will be examples of how to handle different kinds of challenges soon).

## Admitting Your Wrongs Promptly

In step ten, *wrong* has a different meaning than when it was used in the fifth step. In step five, the word referred to moral character defects. In this step, the word refers to whether or not an AA member's behavior is appropriate. One way to define *wrong* is that something isn't proper or that it doesn't meet requirements.

In this process of recovery, the concept of wrong works like this: If your plan becomes not proper enough to help you stay abstinent while you deal with a particular problem, then your plan is wrong for that problem. That means your plan is not in *accordance* with requirements necessary to help you stay abstinent. So, you need to revise your plan.

If you need to revise your plan, you must admit that you have to do that; do it promptly. Promptly means to act quick. Delay is high-risk behavior. If you delay in revising your plan, then you flirt with relapse. If you encounter a new challenge, beyond what your plan can help you handle, then admit it quickly, and figure out a way to handle it.

# How to Know Your Plan Isn't Proper

You may find that your plan of action isn't proper for a variety of reasons. It all boils down to this: When your plan of action, as it is right now, can't help you handle a problem so that you can stay abstinent, then your plan is lacking. That's when you need to revise and improve it.

Sometimes you may need to revise your plan almost as quickly as you begin it. This happens in the event that an everyday situation creates an unanticipated threat to your abstinence. For example, suppose you said that you should avoid a certain place where you had always used or drank. Now, suppose when you made your plan of action you overlooked the fact that when you walk to work you pass by that certain place. If your plan doesn't include a way to deal with that, then you must promptly change your plan. You need to get to work using a different route.

Brian, a patient of mine seeming to do well in his recovery, discovered by surprise that his plan needed some speedy revising. Brian's primary addiction was to crystal methamphetamine, but he had tried just about every abusable drug there was. Often, he'd try something new or different, but end the experience with batu. Some of his experiences included inhalants—that is, inhaling the vapor of something to experience a feeling of euphoria and possibly hallucinate.

Brian, by profession, trained people in sales skills. His technique included writing things on a board for emphasis. On his second day back at the job after treatment, he gave a presentation. He wrote some of his points on a grease board using special dry-erase markers. The markers he used gave off a harsh vapor similar to some of the solvents Brian had used during his drug-using days. He actually found it hard to concentrate on his presentation as soon as he took the cap off the first pen he was using. He said it wasn't like he felt like using right at that moment, but he kept thinking about the vapor, and that made him think about his drug-using past. He thought if he didn't discuss it with someone, then he'd never get it off his mind and would probably relapse before the end of the week.

Brian brought the issue to that night's group-therapy session. He hadn't realized how risky he might consider those pens. He needed to include a plan of action to reduce that risk. Brian decided the easiest thing to do would be to use chart paper and watercolor markers rather than the pens and board. It might be clumsy at times, but Brian said it was worth his recovery. He would also let a few of his co-workers in on his dilemma—several of their names were on his list of sources of support. If there were times he absolutely had to use the dry-erase markers, then he'd make sure a colleague kept the pens before and after the presentation, and then he'd discuss how he was feeling about his recovery with one of his sources of support.

There will be other times when your plan of action is challenged in more substantial ways. Consider the following examples which will offer unexpected challenges, followed by a discussion of resolutions in a separate section coming up.

## Relationship Turmoil

You may realize, six months after your started your abstinence and recovery, that you feel dissatisfied with the way you and your partner communicate. You argue, fight, and accuse each other a lot more than you talk and work things out with each other. Although this problem may have gone on for years, you've now stayed abstinent for a while and you think more clearly. You can recognize the problem as a problem. Perhaps the problem led to months of frustration for you, and you have sometimes thought about using or drinking to help relieve some of that frustration.

After several attempts at discussing things, and even suggesting counseling, your partner tells you in no uncertain terms that he or she blames you for everything. Your partner says that if anyone needs counseling it's you and you alone. Your partner says that ever since you began recovery you haven't been the same person. Your partner is satisfied with the way you both communicate, and tells you that if you don't like it, you should leave.

After thinking it over and discussing it with friends, you decide to leave. You feel sad, lonely, and vulnerable. You don't know exactly what to do, especially because you had made your plan of action assuming that you and your partner would be to-gether forever.

## An Unexpected Personal Crisis

Suppose after a few months into recovery from alcohol de-pendency you have a car accident. As a result, you must take pain pills for two weeks, and when you stop you experience with-drawal symptoms again, and you want a drink like never before. You'll have to miss work for at least five weeks and the bills pile up. A collection agency actually sends you a letter before you get all your stitches removed. You made your plan of action counting on your job and on a steady income. You start to wonder if a "lit-tle something" wouldn't take the edge off your frustration, and help settle your nerves.

## Family Crisis

Suppose after three months of recovery, you suddenly learn an important family member has a terminal illness. You feel afraid, sad, angry. You also feel like maybe you should stop attending your support groups to help this person. You want to help this relative, but you must also maintain your abstinence. Your plan didn't include provisions for anyone's terminal illness.

## A Holiday You Forgot About

Lots of alcohol and drug dependent people begin their re-covery with a plan of action that works fine during "normal" days. Then a "special" event comes up—something that regularly occurs—and neither their plan of action, nor they, are prepared for it.

Birthdays are a good example. The holidays between Hal-loween and New Year's Eve are worse. Other examples include Super Bowl Sunday, any three-day weekend and any day full of unexpected free time, like a sick day when you're not really sick.

These are high-risk days because your plan of action may not have included ways for you to deal with them. Right now, do you know how you're going to spend this coming New Year's Eve?

# How to Adjust Your Plan

In each of these situations, your plan needs a boost. You should admit this quickly and get to work making changes on your plan. How do you change your plan? Start making a change that will help you solve your new challenge but also help you stay drug and alcohol-free. Whenever necessary, ask your sources of support for their input.

As you make your changes and ask for advice from your sources of support, consider the following:

- Maybe you should expand on part of your plan of action.

- Perhaps it would help if you went to more support groups for a while.

- Perhaps you should become more involved in free-time activities that can help you abstain.

- Maybe you should plan your current free-time activities more carefully, right now.

- Maybe you should return to the therapist who helped you begin recovery; maybe you could use a few booster sessions.

- Maybe you should spend some extra time with a source of support. Maybe you should just make arrangements to call a source of support and give daily updates on how you're handling the new challenge.

- Maybe there is a place on your high-risk list that you should especially not go to at this fragile time?

Are there new developments in your life that require you to add to your plan? Consider possible solutions for the following questions:

- Should you find a different kind of support group, one that specifically helps with the problem you're now facing?

- Should you come up with some new activities to do?

- Should you avoid certain people or things you hadn't thought of before?

Think of some possible solutions to these three examples.

## Changing Your Plan to Deal with Relationship Turmoil

Remember the earlier example, where you need to leave your partner? What are your options for that dilemma? You might contact a shelter. You might hire an attorney to help you protect yourself and your possessions. Can you stay with someone for a few days until you get your feet on the ground? Think of how you should look for a new place to stay. Can you check the classified ads in a paper? A neighborhood posting? A placement service?

Can you afford your own place? Does your current job provide you with enough income? Do you need to look for a new job, or ask your current employer what you need to do to get a raise? Can you trust your partner to handle this well, or should you contact the police to ask for advice? You really need to get extra support from your sources of support. Who can you talk to about all this? Should you go to any extra support groups to help keep up your stamina?

Making these kinds of decisions and changes will help you solve your unexpected relationship turmoil, in turn helping you stay abstinent despite the new challenges.

## Changing Your plan to Deal with Unexpected Personal Crisis

In the case of the second example in which you've had a car accident, how could you make your plan stronger? Who can help you with the withdrawal symptoms? Who of your sources of support have gone through withdrawal symptoms too? Could the doctor who gave you the drugs help you? Name your friends and support group members who will understand your cravings and then call them up.

What kind of activities or projects can you involve yourself in to keep your mind occupied? Is the collection agency willing to reason with you? Who can you complain to about the collection agency (a government agency, a supervisor at the collection agency)? Do you have friends or relatives that you can ask to have you over for dinner so you don't have to worry about at least the cost of one meal this week? You can offer to return the favor as soon as you're more financially stable.

## Changing Your Plan to Deal with Family Crisis

In a situation where a sick relative needs your attention, you need to be careful as you alter your plan. You may in fact need to free up some of your time to spend more time with the relative. This might mean not attending as many support group meetings or counseling sessions. Still, you must keep yourself active in your recovery program. This is when you need to adjust your plan to fit the unexpected event.

Perhaps you could make arrangements with your sources of support to telephone them more often during this temporary new crisis. This way you could make up for the support you lose by not attending meetings. That would be a good revision to your plan.

You'll also need to make plans for some extra time to allow yourself to feel upset and blow off some steam during this new and difficult situation, but still not use or drink. Who can you call? Who can you talk with? Should you plan for some other physical activity to help rejuvenate yourself? Are there healthier members in your family with whom you can discuss your feelings, and get respect for your need to abstain?

## Changing Your Plan to Deal with Holidays

Fortunately, your plan of action should never have this problem more than once. After you improve your plan for the first holiday, keep those changes in place for future holidays.

By this time, you probably have the hang of how you'd change your plan. Where should you go so you can celebrate and stay abstinent? With whom should you celebrate? Who could you invite to celebrate with you—without using or drinking. Can you arrange to celebrate with people you've met in your support groups? How much notice do you need to deal with future holidays or your birthday?

# Secondary Recovery Issues

As your time in recovery goes on, you will need to deal with the other issues in your life that you put off earlier in your recovery. Those other issues make up the secondary recovery issues like personal, self-esteem, or childhood issues. If you still want to work on these areas of your life, you now have a better chance to do so successfully without relapse.

You've been focusing strictly on your recovery up until this point. Now comes the time when you can work on changing your emotional life, or your personal and intimate relationships. Perhaps you feel that it is time for you to work on family of origin issues or past traumas. You can even work on financial and career changes; just make sure your first priority will still be to continue your plan of action to stay abstinent while you work on these issues.

No matter when or what the issue, understand that you shouldn't feel obligated to address an issue unless you want to. You very well could have something in your memory that someone *else* would think of as a problem worth exploring. However, if you don't, then don't force yourself. If it's not bothering you or your recovery, you don't have to deal with it.

To deal with these issues successfully, involve a source of support to help you. You haven't been able to resolve these issues by yourself so far; don't expect that your abstinence will make you a personal expert at these issues now. Find some help for you to deal with these issues. Find a therapist, a knowledgeable helper, a very good friend, or a counselor of some kind. Find a professional. Find a support group.

As you do this work, give yourself some time. Exploring and working on secondary recovery issues may be quite involved. The more complex the issue, the more time, patience, and work you'll need to put into solving it. You will not resolve issues of childhood trauma, for example, in a matter of a few hours' work with a good friend. You may have many complex issues you want to deal with. You may have just a few. Work on them as you feel ready. Use the concepts of this goal to help you do it. Improve your whole life, and make sure this also improves your recovery. Be sure to adjust your plan accordingly—realize that working on these issues will be emotionally disturbing and you may need extra support to help with your abstinence.

## How to Revise Your Plan

On another piece of paper or in your journal, write the three statements shown in the example beginning on the next page.

Now, answer them. You can start your answers in this book and continue in your journal.

First, write down what the new problem is that your current plan of action doesn't help you solve well, and therefore could threaten your abstinence. Then, write down how or why it threatens your abstinence. What should you do about it? Discuss this with some of your sources of support. When you come up with a solution, write it down also. As always, check your answers with some of your sources of support.

You have now updated and improved your plan of action. Now act on your revised plan. You can think of this goal as refining the "rough draft" of your plan you wrote in chapter 7. This means, review your whole process up to this point in order to help you keep your abstinence in new situations that you hadn't prepared for in your original plan. Here are some suggestions for how to review your process so far:

- Diagnose the problem threatening your abstinence (similar to making your self-diagnosis in goal one).

- Identify how you need to change to protect your abstinence (goals two and three).

- Figure out how to solve the problem (goals four and five).

- Develop a plan of action (goal six).

- Do it (goal seven).

Act on your updated plan, now. Put it to work. If it needs even more revising, then revise it some more. Make sure your plan will help you solve your problem but still help you stay abstinent.

## Changes to My Plan of Action

**I have identified this new problem as having the ability to threaten my recovery:**

**Here is how it could threaten my abstinence:**

**Here is what I will do to overcome this newly recognized problem while still protecting my abstinence:**

# Recognize Your Success!

This goal goes further than just solving new problems. You need to think about the positive as well as the negative aspects of your recovery. As you evaluate your plan in this goal, give yourself some credit for areas that don't need revision. You gave your plan a lot of thought and hard work. If you have chemical dependency and are sticking to your recovery plan and avoiding relapse, you deserve a pat on the back! Recovery, which involves intense lifestyle changes, is tough. Don't take your success lightly.

Many people who try abstinence and recovery don't make it. The first six months are the most difficult. The next six are easier, but you're not out of the woods yet. Although your second year is easier, you still might need to do a lot of revision on your plan of action. If you can make it two years, you've got a great chance of making it forever.

Making it through that first six months is hard. Don't take your success for granted when you end another day still abstinent. Praise yourself for your successful time in recovery. You'll enjoy your recovery more if you remember to do that than if you only think about the problems and the changes you need to make. You should always do both.

Cinda's situation is an example of how much it can mean to simply notice how much time you've had in recovery. She had worked a recovery plan diligently for some time. She improved her job performance, several of her relationships, and had begun to exercise and feel better about the way she looked. She attributed all this to the fact that she had avoided alcohol. She had regularly attended a support group, had made friends there, and had been a support to several women and even a few men who had come to the group. The problem was that for two weeks, she had begun to feel a little depressed over all the work that she felt recovery was taking for her to continue to succeed. She was afraid she was falling into a rut, and she wondered if she wasn't losing some of her commitment to recovery.

She expressed this in group, winding it all up with saying that, while she was happy with her accomplishments as a result of her recovery, she wondered how long it would take before she'd feel good about *being* in recovery. Someone asked her how long she'd been in recovery in the first place. This took her by surprise, and everyone in the group chuckled at the look on her face as she tried to remember back to the first day she began recovery. After a minute, she remembered that her last drink was two days shy of one year ago. She had gone 363 days without alcohol. She reported this with wide-eyed wonderment and the group burst into applause. Cinda's hard work had paid off in many ways for her, and now that she could praise herself by knowing how long she had worked at it, her recovery was more meaningful. She said she believed that she had never worked as hard in one year to achieve so much.

To praise yourself, you could, for example, simply acknowledge to yourself that you have more sound judgment than you did the day before you began to abstain. Maybe buy yourself a new CD or an ice cream cone and reflect on how well you've done up to this point.

All literature from AA and NA includes praise for improved lives and lifestyles. The membership of almost any recovery group will take time to applaud members who can claim any length of time in recovery, especially a milestone like one month, ninety days, or a year. Call it an anniversary, call it a birthday, but if it will bring you a sense of accomplishment, call it—you deserve it.

# Reaching Your Eighth Goal

With this goal, you evaluate your relapse-prevention plan and change it where you need to. You also give yourself credit for maintaining your abstinence and therefore your sound judgment. Here's the therapeutic statement for this goal:

*I evaluate my progress, praising myself as appropriate, and changing my plan when necessary.*

You will be doing the process of this goal over and over for a long time. In fact, you will work on this goal and the next two for the rest of your lifetime. These last three goals will help you improve your lifestyle in many different ways. Remember, recovery is a process not an event. By maintaining your abstinence, you're maintaining a lifetime of improvement. You might realize, as you evaluate your plan, that a certain problem proves too complex for the sources of support you already identified and now have at your service. You might need to find a new source of support. The next goal will help you search for and select new sources of support. Time to move on.

# 9

## Identify New Sources of Support

As you gain more time in recovery, say, after half a year, you will probably discover that those people and things you listed as your sources of support don't always have the ability to help you solve your newly realized problems. This goal, working closely with the eighth goal, will help you find new sources of support. These new sources will help you solve new problems, strengthening your abstinence and your recovery even more. By this time, you should be practicing a strong and solid recovery. You've been successful at solving some unexpected challenges while remaining drug- and alcohol-free. This goal will help you strengthen your recovery even more.

Your ninth goal uses the important concepts from the eleventh step of Alcoholics Anonymous, which reads, "Sought through prayer and meditation to improve our conscious contact with God *as we understood Him,* praying only for knowledge of His will for us and the power to carry that out." First we'll look at the important concepts from the first part of the step. The second half of this step, "praying only for knowledge of His will for us and the power to carry that out," makes up another concept.

## "God" and "Him"

Remember the concept behind the words *God* and *Him*. Once again, this therapeutic process translates the concept of "God" into "sources of support." You can name whoever or whatever you want as long as you can use them to help you abstain.

## "Sought" and "Improve"

*Sought* means to try to discover something or to try to acquire or gain something. For the purposes of this process, the word means you need to continue learning more in order to successfully maintain your recovery.

*Improve* means to make something better. These concepts combined mean that you need to find out how to make your sources of support better. You need to seek out more information to improve your recovery.

## Conscious Contact

To be *conscious* of something is to be aware of that thing. To be in *contact* with something means to be very close to it. This goal will help you become more aware of what other sources of support you have close to you. You may have a source of support available to you that you don't even realize could be there for you, even though you could be sitting right beside it!

Put all this together: With this goal, you'll seek out new ways to learn to improve your awareness of what or who could be a source of support for you. You need to find out about new sources of support so you can improve your chances to maintain your abstinence and strengthen your recovery. This goal challenges you to find new sources of support when the need arises. How do you do this? Don't worry, you'll soon be given useful suggestions for ways to accomplish this goal.

## The Concept Behind Prayer and Meditation

These two terms mean similar things. When you *meditate*, you try to solve a problem through your own calm and centered thought. You *reflect* on your problem and come up with possible solutions until you can settle on some action to take.

*Prayer* can mean simply an entreaty or question. The concept behind this word doesn't have to be a conversation with God. Prayer could be merely asking for something, like advice. For example, you could ask for advice on how to change and strengthen your plan of action even more than you have done so before—"I pray thee, sir, how might I do this even better?"

Early in your recovery, you worked on just maintaining your abstinence. The eighth goal helped you begin to work on the more complicated issues in your life. Some of these issues may not have directly effected your use of drugs or alcohol, at least not at the beginning of your abstinence.

When you were originally creating your list of sources of support, you didn't know you should include people or things that could help you solve these bigger problems. Even though you realize now that you need new sources of support to help you make even bigger improvements on your recovery, you may not know who to add to that list, or even who or what your should look for. This is where prayer and meditation come in, or more appropriately, asking and reflecting. When you need more help than your current sources of support can give you, then you need to ask and to think about where to find new sources of support. Once you find those new sources of support, you need to use them.

## Finding New Sources of Support

You simply need to start looking at your options. Ask around, do some research, and check on some leads. This is similar to the work you did on your second goal, but with an important difference.

With goal two you knew you were dealing with only chemical dependency, a problem for which many people and things were available to you for help. Your chemical dependency was probably known by many people, and these people knew about the hard work you were doing to recover. You talked about it and asked for help from people eager or willing to help you. But now you need more and different kinds of help; so, how exactly do you find new ones?

## New Problems

At this point, again around six months and more after your last drink or use of drugs, you probably have enough stability in your recovery to begin facing some more of your past or current personal concerns. These kinds of issues will be more intense, more troublesome to you than those mentioned in the previous chapter. Now might be the time to begin dealing with the memories you might have over an abusive relationship, abuse you suffered as a child, or other bothersome things that happened to you that you just can't forget. Or now might be the time to discuss some characteristics you have that you can't seem to shake, but that cause you trouble—like a tendency to choose unhealthy people with whom to become involved, or a tendency to sabotage your efforts whenever you try to make healthy changes in your life.

You might want to face up to some health problems you haven't yet dealt with, like quitting smoking or going on a diet. Maybe it's time to own up to some debts, some past financial irresponsibility, or even just a stunning pile of parking tickets. Perhaps it's time to reconnect with family. Maybe you want to settle an outstanding legal problem you've been avoiding.

All of these are examples of situations and personal issues that you could deal with now with more likelihood of success than when you first began recovery. All of these are also examples of situations and issues your current sources of support are probably unable to help you solve. You need to find new sources of support, and this goal can help you with that. Then, the process you learn in this goal can help you do this even into your future recovery. The longer you stay abstinent, the more likely something will come up in your mind that you'll want to work out.

In the future, say after your first anniversary of recovery, you could begin dealing with even more intense issues than the ones mentioned. Perhaps you have a history of suffering severe child abuse or even recurrent sexual assault. Maybe you witnessed a crime or a trauma so devastating that you've never been able to talk about it, even though you wanted to. Maybe you've been enduring a terrible problem all this time that you never thought you could stop. All of these are issues that will require some new sources of support to help you resolve them.

As mentioned in the previous chapter, you should work on these problems only if you think of them as problems. A bad memory isn't always a problem for everyone. If you're not sure if you should work on a particular problem, then ask yourself the following questions:

- Is this issue something you haven't dealt with already to your satisfaction?

- Is the issue something that troubles you a lot?

- Is the issue on your mind so much that it could threaten your abstinence by making you neglect your responsibility to stay abstinent and avoid relapse?

- Is the issue something that you either don't want to discuss with your current sources of support, or something that you're pretty sure those sources of support won't be able to help you overcome?

Any "yes" answer indicates that you're dealing with something for which you ought to get some help. It's important to your continued recovery. In that case, it's time to find a new source of support to help you do that. Here's how to go about that.

## Start with What You've Got

You can probably use your current sources of support to help you find new ones. Those sources may not know how to help you solve your new problems, but you could still use their suggestions to help you find new support. As one source of inspiration, for example, you could talk with friends who have successfully handled problems similar to whatever you might be dealing with now. How did they do it? You could find out by asking them. Were there any people who offered you help before you felt ready to work on these issues? Could those people help you now?

## Find Professional Support

Sometimes you'll need the help of a professional to solve a problem. You might consider whether or not you could contact any of the following resources to help you solve your problem:

- Therapist

- Attorney

- Accountant

- Physician

- Tutor

- Minister

Do you know the kinds of professionals who could help you with your problems? If not, who could you ask to find this out? There are probably professional organizations that can give you a referral. There are often nonprofit organizations willing to help out with various situations if you cannot afford any of these options.

## Other Support Groups

If your problem doesn't require professional guidance, then could you get help from nonprofessional sources of support? Are there any support groups near you that address a secondary recovery issue? There are hundreds of groups of people helping each other for a variety of problems, such as for emotional problems, financial problems, relationship concerns, health matters, and coping skills. The more specific you are when explaining your problem to other people, the more helpful they can be in directing you to a new source of support.

## Be Creative

Only you can limit yourself from finding new sources of support. Ask around, find out who those sources could be.

Be on the look out for advertisements on TV, the radio, or in print. Go to the library and see how many books there are dealing with your problem. Got a computer? Search the Internet for some ideas or even some bulletin boards or chat rooms dealing with your issue. Have you ever heard anyone speak about the problem you have? Try to get in touch with them or with the agency with which they're affiliated. There might be a support group which deals with the problem you have. Contact your local community mental health agency and ask for a referral. Did you see something on a talk show that could help you? Call the TV station and find an address to write for more information.

Even the Yellow Pages can serve as a quick reference guide to sources of support. Let your fingers do the walking through the pages entitled counseling, attorneys, accountants, clergy, mental health, financial services, bail bonds, or other topics until you find a potential source of support.

The following experiences of a few patients will demonstrate when it's important to find a new source of support and how you might go about doing it. The first example is of my patient Sharon. Her story shows that sometimes all you need to do to find new sources is start asking—people will often send you in a new direction if they can't help you.

When Sharon stopped drinking, she began to remember traumatic experiences she had endured as a child. Her drinking had helped her temporarily forget these things. Now, however, the longer she stayed sober, the more she recalled.

She had trusted the guidance of her sources of support who cautioned against exploring those memories too soon. Now, fifteen months sober, Sharon thought it was time to get some additional help. She had spent two months in outpatient treatment, another three months in aftercare, and had been attending her support groups regularly ever since she was discharged from the program. Those memories were always on her mind, and Sharon realized she was beginning to think too much about them. She worried that she was taking time away from thinking about her recovery. She was as committed to her abstinence as ever though, and thought she was ready to handle the additional stress of exploring those emotional issues. Several of her peers in the support group agreed with her.

One of those people told her of a therapist she had seen who seemed to work well for her. Sharon called that therapist. Unfortunately, that therapist wasn't authorized to see patients covered under Sharon's health insurance. However, he gave her the name of two other therapists who he thought were. Sharon called the customer service department of her insurer, who assured her that the two therapists Sharon named were, indeed, preferred providers. Sharon called the first therapist, and discovered that therapist wasn't accepting new patients. That therapist spoke highly of the other therapist. When Sharon called that therapist, she finally connected with someone who was available, respectful of Sharon's need for abstinence, and able to help her deal with her memories.

Sharon's peers and I were impressed with her endurance in finding this therapist. All told, Sharon sought the advice of four people or agencies before finding her new source of support.

Matthew was in his mid-twenties when he pursued recovery. His progress had been rocky; he had relapsed six times in the first fourteen months that he was pursuing recovery. The sixth time landed him in an emergency room, and then into a psychiatric facility. It turned out that Matthew had a mental disorder, a type of schizophrenia, which he had actually been treating, in a crude way, with his use of drugs and alcohol. The disorder made Matthew hear voices inside his head and think that he could see things out of the corner of his eye when there really wasn't anything there. When he used or drank, he was able to calm down those symptoms. Since Matthew had used and drank nearly daily since before the days when these symptoms began to appear, everyone—even Matthew—had just chalked up his unusual thoughts and behavior to his drug use.

While at the facility, Matthew said he really did want to remain abstinent, but didn't see how he could do it if it meant having to deal with the psychotic symptoms. Matthew needed medication that could curtail the psychotic symptoms while still respecting his need to recover. A psychiatrist and I worked together to provide a treatment plan that would allow him to treat the schizophrenia while continuing with his plan of action. Matthew needed this additional support, or else he'd never be able to maintain his abstinence.

In addition to the newfound support of the psychiatrist, Matthew needed to find support that would encourage him to treat his schizophrenia. Matthew found that some of the members of his chemical dependency recovery support group were suspicious of his need for medication. Matthew needed to find the members of the group who could understand his need to treat both his conditions. He also found a support group for schizophrenics, but then needed to find people in that group who would respect his need to not drink or use drugs. It was challenging for him, but Matthew was able to find the sources of support he needed to make the most of his recovery plan.

Frankie, after ten months of good recovery, decided he needed to look for a new source of support of an entirely different kind. Frankie, during his drug-using days, had neglected to file any state or federal income tax for ten years. He believed he needed to resolve that situation and work out a payment plan with the IRS so he could free his conscience and not have any problems if he applied for Social Security benefits.

Understandably fearful, Frankie first sought the advice of an attorney who provided services to the public once a week through a local television station. After that, he made an appointment to talk with agents from both the state tax office and the IRS. Throughout all this groundwork, he gave updates to his friends who knew about his recovery. Everyone encouraged him for taking this big step toward making his life better.

Frankie took along a tape recorder to both interviews. The agents listened to his explanation, helped make sense over his finances and overdue taxes, and worked out a plan to help him whittle down his balance over the course of several years. Frankie wasn't as upset by it all as he thought he might have been. He said when he considered all the new sources of support he sought—the attorney and the two tax agents—he thinks the tape recorder provided him with the best support possible in this situation. It seemed to make things go particularly smooth at the tax offices.

Hanna's need for a new source of support was also unexpected, but not as much a problem. Hanna lived in a special facility for women with newborn children. She progressed well through the residential and outpatient parts of the program, and became ready to pursue employment. Hanna had become so used to the structure and support of the treatment program that she forgot about needing child care so she could work. She didn't realize it until the night before and she had to cancel her first day of employment. Fortunately, her new boss was understanding, and Hanna spent two days interviewing prospective baby-sitters. Once she found a sitter she could trust, she started work. That sitter was another part of Hanna's support—and the sitter didn't even know it.

# The Exception to the Rule: New Sources Must Help You Stay Abstinent

The final concept from the eleventh step gives you one last important thing to remember—it suggests the AA member seek to improve contact with God, "praying only for knowledge of His will for us and the power to carry that out."

The therapeutic recovery process in this book provides you with the knowledge you need to become abstinent and stay that way. Any source of support you find should support you in that overall goal. Anything shy of this will not serve your best interests, and could cause you to relapse.

As you try to solve new problems, you must remember that maintaining your abstinence should be more important to you than anything else. The therapeutic meaning of the phrase "Praying only for the knowledge of His will for us and the power to carry that out" is this: As you seek new sources of support, you should make sure they will not only guide you to solve your other problems, but that they will also always respect your need to stay abstinent. Therefore, you have one limitation in finding new sources of support: **Those new sources must respect your need to stay abstinent.**

This might give you a little trouble at first because while you might find many new potential sources of support, you need to separate those who can help you stay abstinent from those who cannot. Concerned others, other recovering people, sometimes AA or NA members, and even professionals in related fields may not automatically provide the best guidance for your advanced recovery.

I have had patients discover, to their disappointment, that someone they admired and asked for help had a bigger drug problem than they ever had. One patient decided to attend a support group for a health problem, only to discover that everyone always went out for alcoholic drinks at the end of the meeting. Some patients have felt real distress as they try to explain why they can't use drugs to a new source of support who doesn't understand either chemical dependency or recovery. Here are some things to think about when you're evaluating whether or not a possible source of support can really help you.

## Beware of Unhelpful Advice

You will find that lots of potential sources of support will give you advice. However, not all of that advice will be good for you. A friend or counselor who says there isn't any such thing as chemical dependency, or that your don't have it, will not provide good support for you, even if that person seems helpful in other ways. You would probably end up trying to defend your self-diagnosis of chemical dependency, and eventually feel very frustrated and maybe even wonder if any of this person's opinion is helpful. You could end up doubting all the work you did to come to terms with your self-diagnosis and your plan of action. Eventually, frustrated, you might even give up on your abstinence.

## Beware of Being Tempted to Give Up on Your Recovery Program

You also don't need the confusion that you might experience over someone who says you would cure your chemical dependency as soon as you made an effort to improve some other area of your life. This kind of advice ignores the fact that you would have your chemical dependency whether or not your life was perfect. *Powerlessness and unmanageability over drugs or alcohol are not the results of a bad life.* Even if your life were dramatically improved tomorrow, you still couldn't control how much you used or drank or the consequences if you used or drank.

Therefore, avoid and ignore the advice of people who tell you that you would solve your chemical dependency "as soon as you met the right girl," "got the right job," "won the lottery," "got your alimony payments raised," "left your religion," or "sued the bastard." This won't cure your chemical dependency. It could, however, make you so anxious over trying to make that kind of cure work that you'd forget all about the real work you needed to do to stay abstinent.

You'll find no real support from someone who says drug dependency is really an issue of willpower, and you just don't have any. You will not overcome your powerlessness and unmanageability by becoming a more assertive individual. That will only make you a chemically dependent person who's really assertive.

Someone who disregards your need to stay abstinent will not give you good support either. Well-meaning people who encourage you to have "just one," or use or drink "a little just this one time," will not help you the way you need help. You need the help of someone who respects your need to remain abstinent.

## Beware of Those Who Are Unsupportive of Your Abstinence

You will not receive help from people who criticize you because of your abstinence. Perhaps you've already had to deal with people who have said, "Look at you, now you've gotten clean and you think you're better than the rest of us," or, "You think you need to not use or drink, but that's just a lot of bull. Why do you believe the things they say at that treatment program?"

Again, this is the sign of someone who doesn't understand chemical dependency or recovery. It's also a sign of someone who probably has a problem of their own with drugs or alcohol. Don't look for help from those people. Find someone else who could guide and support you in your abstinence.

## Beware of the Recovering People Who Are Judgmental of Your Plan of Action

Sometimes, potential sources of support may not really understand your problems or how your problems should be solved. For example, members at support group meetings will sometimes criticize you if you seek medical or psychiatric treatment. If you talk about your need for therapy or your need to take medications to help cope with a mental disorder or depression, you may find that certain members of a meeting judge you for taking those drugs.

Some "hard-liners" in recovery groups insist that the goals of any recovery program must include an absolute no-drugs policy. Those people will not help you if you ask them for their support. You shouldn't try to seek their support; you'll just end up either confused about your need to use these helpful medications, or you'll resent the members for criticizing you. Either way, you would probably get more upset than get help.

You may find that some recovering people criticize you for wanting to examine other personal issues. This sometimes occurs when the other person, who had the same problem, decided to deal with it differently than you. Don't alter your recovery program based on their advice; your program of recovery is different than their program. If your program keeps you abstinent, then it works for you.

## Beware of People Who Want You to Use Different Drugs

Your recovery will also suffer if you try to take the advice from someone who says you can overcome your chemical dependency by using abusable drugs. Beware of the person or professional who says something like, "I know you've had a problem with drugs, but you're so tense and upset now, why don't you just take a little of this tranquilizer—just half the pill, even. I'll give you just enough to last you a week. See that you don't use more than this, and next week I'll give you some more. Take this every six hours, or whenever you feel tense. We don't even have to tell anyone you're doing this. Go ahead. It works wonders for me. It works wonders for other people."

This is the sign of someone who doesn't understand the overriding nature of chemical dependency. If you, a chemically dependent person, use drugs that you could abuse, and you get to control how you use the drugs, then you will eventually abuse them. Maybe not immediately, but eventually.

When you begin working on your emotional problems, you'll become anxious. It's natural for you to feel anxiety when you're in therapy or when you try to solve issues that you may find difficult to revisit. Anxiety isn't something bad, it's just part of confronting deep-seated problems in your life. So, whatever you do, don't threaten your abstinence by using alcohol or by using drugs that you can abuse.

However, there is an exception to this rule. If a doctor who understands chemical dependency says you need to take a certain medication for a certain problem, then take the drugs. Talk with the doctor about how you feel about the drugs, and make sure the doctor and you work out a safe plan to help you take the drugs.

For example, you might decide to get only a three-day supply of the drugs at a time. This might seem inconvenient for you, or for the doctor, but it might be better for you to do that than to have a month's supply of a high-risk drug calling to you from your medicine cabinet.

# New Sources of Support: What to Look For

Make sure the people or organizations from which you seek help really can help you. If they cannot help you, then do not try to rely on them for help. Find other, helpful, new sources of support. Here are some ways to identify new, healthy sources of support.

## Appropriate Training

Your new sources of support should have the appropriate training to deal with your needs. For example, a psychiatrist and an AA sponsor may both have equal knowledge about recovery issues. The psychiatrist, however, has training about medications to relieve depression for you; the AA sponsor does not. A therapist and a really good friend may both have valuable personal experience in recovery. The therapist, however, has the legal obligation to keep what you say confidential, as well as the training on how to help you solve intimate personal issues. Your really good friend may not.

## Nonprofessionals

Of course, a nonprofessional may be able to help you more than a professional in some ways. You'll have easier access to a member of a support group or a trusted companion than you will to a professional. A sponsor will promise to help you even after office hours; most professionals do not.

As you examine some of your more personal issues, you might experience painful emotions. As mentioned, this is normal. The support of someone outside an office who can sit beside you while you cry for a long time will sometimes help you more than a professional who may need to ask you to pull yourself together in time for the session to end.

Some people may not understand the kinds of problems you experience. Some may not understand why you'd want to talk about these kinds of things in the first place. If you believe you need some help, don't try to convince someone else of it. Find someone who knows about the kinds of things you want to solve. Then talk with that person and follow that person's advice if you trust that it's going to help you. This person becomes a new source of support for you.

Following your new source of support's advice means you've revised your plan of action. Your plan is then working better than before.

## Identifying Your New Problem and Sources of Support

Time now to put all this together. Time to name the new challenge to your recovery, the source of support you've identified, and how you hope that source will help you.

On the next page, a separate piece of paper, or in your journal write out your newest problem, why you need new sources of support, and then develop a strategy to improve your plan of action even further. As you work on this, think of how you would answer these:

- What new problem have you identified?

- What makes this a new problem—that is, why didn't you know about it when you were writing your original plan of action?

- Why does it threaten your abstinence?

- How would this new problem lead you to relapse if you just didn't do anything about it?

- Who can help you overcome this new problem?

- Where or to whom can you go to find out who can help you?

- When you find a new source of support, how can the new source help you solve this new problem?

- Who can help you more with this new problem—a trained professional or a friend?

- What will you need to do to solve this problem and still stay abstinent?

- What will be your new plan of action to solve this problem and still protect your recovery?

Check you answers to these questions with your new source of support. When it seems like your new sources of support can help you, then give them the chance and use them.

## Exercise: Drafting a New Plan
## Using a New Source of Support

I have identified this new problem as a threat to my abstinence:

_____

_____

I have identified the following people or things which could help me overcome this new problem (new sources of support):

_____

_____

They could help me overcome this problem in this way:

_____

_____

I will use these new sources of support to improve my plan of action and help me overcome this problem in this way:

_____

_____

Say for instance you decided that in all your life, you've never had a satisfying long-term relationship. You realize that this problem could affect your recovery because the overwhelming feelings of loneliness make it hard to feel good about any improvements you make on yourself. You search for a new source of support, and decide to seek counseling from a therapist working at a local not-for-profit mental health center in town. You want this therapist to help you understand why you have these relationship problems. So, you decide to attend individual and group counseling services until the therapist and you decide you've had enough to make the kinds of improvements in your life you need to make. All the preliminary information would go on the worksheet. It gives you focus for your continued improvement. If you take your answers to your therapist on your first appointment, it will give the therapist a good idea of what kinds of improvements you've been making, and what you want to achieve by being in therapy now.

### Be Patient

The kinds of problems you're now ready to try and deal with might create big challenges for you to stay abstinent. Don't expect to solve any of these deep personal problems quickly. This kind of work is supposed to be difficult. Remember, however, you'll succeed at the work as long as you have found appropriate sources of support to help you, and as long as you follow their guidelines that help you both solve the problem and keep from using drugs or alcohol.

Doing this work will flavor the rest of your recovery. When you do this work with the right kind of support, you'll find any future work you need to do will be much easier.

# Reaching Your Ninth Goal

This goal helps you find new sources of support who will help you deal with the new problem issues that might come up as you continue your recovery from weeks to months to years. Here is the ninth goal statement for this therapeutic process:

> *I identify and use new sources of support who can help me overcome new problems.*

After you have used this goal and the previous goal for a while, you'll find that this process becomes more familiar to you. Eventually, *the* process of recovery becomes *your* process of recovery. Maintaining your abstinence will become so familiar it will seem automatic for you; it will become your basic nature.

This leaves one more goal.

# 10

## Declare Your Recovery

After some time—longer than a year, and usually even longer than that—you will notice that you have begun to practice your recovery without having to think about it. You haven't used drugs or alcohol in a long time. You naturally avoid high-risk situations. You recognize when you're thinking or feeling high-risk thoughts or attitudes, and you always take action to counteract those head games. You've had success finding new sources of support, as well as meeting and overcoming new challenges to your recovery. Most importantly, your recovery is something that is a part of your lifestyle. It's not something you're constantly trying to remember to do. At that point, your recovery has become a permanent part of your life. This goal will help you determine when you've achieved this state of mind and give you some pointers on never losing your abstinence again.

This tenth goal wraps up your work. You will transition into this goal easily. This goal, like the previous two, deals with other areas in your life besides the practical steps for staying abstinent. While all the goals are a part of your recovery, these last three help you on a more personal or emotional level than just staying abstinent. If you have made it this far, then you have a great chance of lasting recovery.

This final goal uses concepts found in the twelfth step of AA: "Having had a spiritual awakening as the result of these steps, we tried to carry this message to alcoholics, and to practice these principles in all our affairs." A few terms from this step are important to the concepts for this goal.

## "A Spiritual Awakening"

Alcoholics Anonymous, and other twelve step programs, are "spiritual" programs. Many people have trouble understanding the difference between "spiritual" and "religious." This is understandable, because the difference is subtle.

A religion is an organization that promotes certain important ideas or dogma, which are based upon certain spiritual beliefs. A religion can't exist without spirituality, much like a cake needs eggs and flour for it to be a cake. But eggs and flour can stand alone. Spiritual ideas and beliefs do not need a religion in order to have meaning for a believer.

The founders of AA wanted members to develop a personal understanding of how they should get and stay sober. The Twelve Steps create a spiritual, not religious or dogmatic way to do just that. The founders of AA believed that such a personal spiritual interest in recovery would help people more than any particular religion. When they referred to *spiritual* this alluded to something called *spirit*. What does this concept mean? Among other things, it means *the soul as separable from the body at death*. The concept refers to something beyond anything living or physical. If the body dies, the spirit remains.

The concept as it relates to this goal means something about yourself that lasts longer than some other part of you. Your *recovery* is something that *lasts longer than your chemical dependency*. That is, when your recovery and abstinence are solid, it lasts longer than your active use of drugs or alcohol. So, the concept for this goal means that your recovery is lasting. It's not being forced on you, like a religion. It's something you embrace and abide by. It is stronger and will last longer than your use of drugs or alcohol.

*Awakening*, which was used in the original twelfth step, can be defined as "something which makes you aware," much like *awake* means "to wake up, or become aware." The concept of the term *spiritual awakening*, for this process, refers to *you becoming aware of how you can stay abstinent.* With the last nine therapeutic goals, you developed an awareness about how to maintain your abstinence. With this goal, that awareness becomes a permanent part of your lifestyle.

When your dependency goes into remission, that is, as long as you avoid relapse, then your recovery and abstinence remain. Your abstinence will outlast your dependency as long as you remember to keep aware of your recovery in all you do; meaning that when you become aware of your recovery, you should practice the principles of recovery in all your affairs.

### *"Practice" and "Affairs"*

This goal assumes you're capable of practicing your recovery as a full-time commitment. In this case, *practice* doesn't mean something you still have to learn, like practicing your piano lessons so that you'll eventually know how to play the piano. At this point, you practice your recovery as a *habit*, permanently, like practicing sound judgment in all your affairs. This definition is similar to a doctor practicing medicine.

Your *affairs* are those day-to-day things that need your attention. You need to stay aware of your recovery in all your affairs. In other words, in all the matters of your life requiring your action or attention, you need to consider your recovery first. When you do this automatically, or when it becomes your basic nature, then you're practicing permanent recovery and you have permanently returned to having sound judgment.

## Declaring a Strong Recovery

This goal allows you to declare that your recovery is strong. Of course, you won't get to this point quickly; you won't be able to make this declaration anytime during the first year of your program of recovery. Have patience. Remember, even though your chemical dependency took years to develop, it will not take years to develop your recovery though sometimes it will seem that way!

Every day that you maintain your recovery, you strengthen your ability to remain abstinent. Over time, you'll feel less and less threat to your abstinence, and notice fewer and fewer feelings that would make you want to relapse. Remember, it will take many months, perhaps years, before you feel that comfortable.

Recovery from chemical dependency means permanent lifestyle change. Developing and living a new lifestyle, one that is rid of many things you'd grown accustomed to, won't feel quite right for a while. Eventually, you will come to call that new lifestyle yours without regrets or reservations. It will feel familiar and reliable; it will feel like yours.

The story of my patient Amanda shows just how successful life can become as recovery continues over the years. She had used drugs for twenty-five years. She knew how to find drugs, socialized almost exclusively with drug users, and was used to the fast pace and short-term thrill of living the life of an addict and drug dealer. Amanda began her recovery from alcohol, cocaine, and amphetamines when she was forty. Her first year of recovery was tough—filled with cravings and insecurity. Everything felt unfamiliar to her. When she was able to announce her first anniversary at her favorite NA meeting, everyone knew what an effort she had made.

After that first year, Amanda decided to pursue a college degree. She also switched careers, choosing to work with other addicts at a local treatment program. She met and married a healthy man. She improved her relationship with her children and became a positive influence on them to stop their own drug use. At different times in her recovery, she has chosen to pursue therapy to deal with self-esteem, trauma, and relationship issues. She has helped other addicts recover both as a professional and as a sponsor in NA. Twelve years after she began her abstinence, she is a vital part of the local recovery community, respected by other professionals in the field, loved by her friends, happy to be drug-free, and always finding new ways to improve her outlook. Throughout the years Amanda has used the principles of the recovery process outlined in this book to overcome possible relapse triggers, find new sources of support, and keep improving herself and her life.

## How Long Does It Take?

How long it will take you to progress to a point in your recovery when you feel comfortable and used to your abstinence depends on various things. No two people achieve recovery in the same way or at the same time; however, research suggests the following things about how long your recovery might take.

*Women are more likely to stay completely abstinent for the first year than men.* However, more men attempt recovery than women.

*The less emotional stress in the first year of your recovery, the better.* Having more stability in your life at the beginning of your treatment helps. This includes such things as having a family, a job, and steady, decent finances. Of course, you can still succeed at recovery even without that kind of stability. You reviewed these issues when you first developed your plan, and you need to continue to as you revise your plan.

*If you can stay abstinent for six months, you will probably remain abstinent for a whole year.* If you can stay abstinent for two years, you have an excellent chance for a lifetime of abstinence and recovery.

No one can predict the kind of recovery you will have, or how long it will take you to feel comfortable with your recovery. Simply put, it will take as long as it takes. Try to not compare your progress with someone else's; it's not fair to yourself. As long as you stay abstinent, you are doing excellent.

After many years of practicing your program and maintaining abstinence, your program will have become so automatic that you hardly notice it as a "recovery program." At that point, you will hardly have any chance of relapsing, unless something devastating happens in your life. Fortunately you will have a solid plan of action in place for support when unexpected events do come up. Don't assume too early that you're beyond needing a strict plan yet, however. That kind of security usually takes a decade or more of abstinence.

## The End of Recovery: Are We There Yet?

Does your responsibility to maintain a recovery program ever end? The answer is no. You have no finish line for your recovery. Most likely, you won't always need to practice as vigorous a program as you do when you first start. Eventually you could reduce or maybe even stop attending support groups, professional counseling, or avoiding certain people. Of course you'd never do this until after allowing enough years for your recovery to become absolutely solid.

You will always have to maintain your lifestyle so that you cannot return to drinking or drug use again. In that respect, your recovery, your abstinence, your sound judgment, and your lifestyle changes are lifelong responsibilities. Recovery never ends.

## The End of Sources of Support: Am I On My Own Yet?

You're maintaining recovery when you maintain the lifestyle changes which helping to keep you abstinent. Once those lifestyle changes have become a permanent part of your life—your basic nature—then you won't need as much outside help. You can think about whether or not you can decrease your outside help when after a couple of years you

- Feel secure in your abstinence

- Demonstrate sound judgment in everything you do

- View relapsing as a possibility rather than a threat

If you decide, for example, not to attend as many support group meetings or as much therapy, you may still choose to always maintain some participation in those activities. You just won't go as often.

Anytime you decide to significant reduce or all together discontinue some recovery activity, make sure you ask yourself these things:

- Have you really gotten as much out of the activity for your recovery as you possibly can?

- Are you considering this because it's what you want to do (as opposed to something that someone else wants you to do)?

- Do you have an alternative to this activity set up so your abstinence can be as solid as it already has been?

- Do you think most people who are successful at recovery discontinue this activity at this point also?

Any "no" answer is a sign that you're thinking of ending this activity too early. Go discuss your thoughts with one of your sources of support. It's important to your recovery. Otherwise, you'll risk relapse.

You might maintain less contact with certain sources of support, but you need to always keep these people and things available to you—just in case. You also may find that some of your sources of support have become true friends rather than mere support for your abstinence; that's good too. For a recovering person, there's no friend like a sober friend. Furthermore, you should always check your reasoning with at least one of your sources of support if you feel ready to reduce your recovery activities. You might want to reduce your recovery activities too soon, and risk relapsing without realizing it. For example, say you've attended a sobriety support group for thirteen months. For the last four months, you've gone only once a week. All's been well, but now you decide you've done all you need to there, and you can stop attending your groups all together. Are you sure this is wise? Better check that with someone.

First of all, if you don't want to discuss it with someone, you're engaging in high-risk behavior. You shouldn't try to keep secrets from your support. You start to look and act guilty, and you'll eventually avoid them. Furthermore, you won't give yourself the benefit of their input. Find someone to discuss your decision-making over this.

Now, ask yourself if there's any problem with you attending the meeting. Have you really gotten all you possibly can out of the meeting? Is it harming you somehow? Do you have a plan of action set up to help you maintain abstinence without this meeting? If you've answered any of these questions "no," then you should reconsider discontinuing the meetings. You're still getting something out of them. Perhaps you should just try to regain your interest in the meeting.

Do you need to become more involved so you feel more a part of the meetings? Should you find a different meeting of the same organization? Should you find new people to associate with at the meeting? Any of these could make the meetings seem more interesting to you.

Are you engaging in high-risk behavior that's subtle? Losing interest in your meeting might actually be setting yourself up to relapse. You should discuss this with a source of support. Think again of how long you used drugs or drank alcohol; have you really had enough time at recovery to counterbalance all that?

If you've attended a support-group meeting for just over a year, it's not time to stop attending the meeting. Well-functioning support groups will give a benefit to the membership for longer than that. Give it more time, or go find a different support group. Most people find some benefit from a support-group meeting for at least two to seven years, and many never stop feeling the benefit from the meetings. Reconsider whether or not you're getting something out of the meeting in another year. You'll be at less risk if you stop attending later on, but not now.

That's why talking it over with a source of support is so important. Remember that recovery is a process, not an event. You don't practice this process in order to earn an "A" and complete a task. You practice it to develop and maintain an abstinent lifestyle. Recovery is a pass or fail course.

## There Is Something You Don't Have to Do

There is one big difference between this goal and AA's twelfth step. This goal doesn't ask you to "carry this message" to others. While you could feel a sense of reward by doing that, you don't have to in order to maintain your abstinence.

The first meeting of minds that led to the creation of the Twelve Steps occurred on Mothers Day in 1935, when Bill Wilson and Dr. Bob Smith met. They understood then that their style of recovery could work only by alcoholics helping other alcoholics. When AA finally caught on, it did so with a flourish. Suffering people saw AA as a source of face-to-face help. Early in the days of AA, men with fewer than thirty days of sobriety went to help potential new members in the hospital and out on the streets. As some of these people achieved sobriety, AA became popular and earned the respect of many because of their unusual style of outreach.

In the last few decades, however, different processes have also proven effective at promoting recovery. Counseling efforts, behavioral efforts, support groups that don't follow the Twelve Steps, and religious efforts have all contributed to the recovery of addicts and alcohol dependent people. While they all include group support, none of these efforts suggest that a recovering person should help another. Even AA, after its first few years, decided that members should reduce their efforts to draw newcomers into the fold.

Reaching out to help someone in need, especially when you have had similar trouble, can certainly feel rewarding. You have some experience that could help a fellow chemically dependent person in ways that another concerned person couldn't. As noted in chapter 9, you might even be more helpful than a professional counselor or psychiatrist in some ways. If you think helping others will strengthen your ability to avoid relapse, then look into the possibilities of counseling or volunteering.

Most chemical dependency treatment programs have opportunities for volunteers to help out. It might even give you the opportunity to move into a paid position. Otherwise, you could always take a more active role in a support group that you attend, or you could help out at the administrative office with which your support group is affiliated. Perhaps there's a phone hotline you can help staff to answer questions about recovery or local treatment options. If you're a member of AA or NA, you could always help out with those programs' central offices outreach service or twelfth step calls.

No matter what you do, don't try to help another drug or alcohol dependent person in your first year of recovery. In your first year, you really don't know enough about how to stay sober. You stand a good chance of injuring someone else more than helping them. Your emotions are still getting back to normal and you may not be able to handle it if the person you try to help relapses—there's a better chance of that than there is of that person getting better.

Do not make this effort the primary concern in your recovery program, otherwise you'll feel a sense of accomplishment only as a result of someone else's behavior, not your own. This sets you up for a lot of disappointment if the other person doesn't make it. It could discourage or disappoint you so much that you could lose sight of your own need to remain abstinent, and focus instead on trying to "make" someone else remain abstinent—you will relapse if you do that.

Abstinence is hard to maintain. You probably know that, right? Relapse is common. You may get upset over the numbers of relapses you see in other people while you try to help them. Be careful! This disappointment can lead you to high-risk thoughts or attitudes. Help others if you want to, but stay abstinent at all costs. This is your most important goal. If helping others becomes too hard for you, then stop.

## Reaching Your Tenth and Final Goal

The previous nine goals helped you establish a lifestyle based upon not using drugs or alcohol. By reaching these goals, you have overcome your chemical dependency. This goal, in which you acknowledge your efforts have become a permanent part of your lifestyle, is the icing on your cake. You've mastered abstinence. Here is the therapeutic goal statement for this point of your process:

> *Having made satisfying improvements in my sound judgment by using these goals, I continue to make improvements in other areas of my life, as this process has become my basic nature.*

As long as you stick to your plan of action and make improvements on it, then you will *keep your abstinence, keep your recovery, and avoid relapse.* The final three goals blend together at this point. When maintaining your abstinence becomes your basic nature, you can declare your recovery.

**From here on, just keep it up.**

# 11

## Putting It All Together: Pointers for Recovering People

The more information about recovery you have, the better your chances for success. Here are a few last words of caution and encouragement to help you stay in charge of your recovery.

## Recovery Is Your Responsibility

First, keep in mind that you alone always have the responsibility to maintain your abstinence and recovery. Other people and influences may try and take that responsibility from you from time to time. Some may also tell you that you should approach recovery in ways that won't work for you. Regardless of their wishes, your recovery is still yours to figure out.

Perhaps you began your recovery because of other people. Maybe your concerned family and friends had ideas about how you should maintain your abstinence. Employers and legal authorities may have threatened to inflict certain consequences if you relapsed. Or religious and other professionals may predict certain dire results should you return to drug or alcohol use. Those influences can certainly help you find the motivation to begin your recovery process; however, once those influences go away, you may not feel the same motivation. If you want your recovery to last, you have to take responsibility to maintain your abstinence regardless of those outside influences. You cannot stay abstinent to please others; do it to improve your health and lifestyle.

Malia is an unfortunate example of this. Malia began treatment because her husband said he was going to leave her if she didn't. She seemed to make a decent effort at recovery, though complained sometimes about how long it all was taking. After a few weeks, when she was working on goal five, Malia stopped coming. I contacted her at home to ask why. Malia said her husband no longer wanted to leave her, and therefore, she didn't need to continue treatment. Then she hung up the phone without saying good-bye. Clearly, Malia wasn't in treatment for herself, she was there to impress her husband. Unfortunately, six months later, Malia contacted my office again and reported that her husband was "really" going to leave her, this time, if she didn't pursue treatment, again.

You might have started recovery because you want to avoid jail, divorce, breakup, unemployment, or arrest. Of course, those are good reasons to start. However, you will succeed in your recovery only if you continue because you want it for yourself.

## Be Aware of Relapse

As you try to maintain your abstinence, you might have to deal with unexpected opportunities to relapse. You might also decide to take advantage of those opportunities.

Relapse is never appropriate nor will you find it satisfying in the long run. However, many recovering people do relapse, sometimes even more than once in early recovery.

One patient of mine, Tanya, relapsed frequently. She would come into my office, usually without an appointment, and almost always intoxicated. She would say that she had relapsed again and that it was my fault for telling her that she might relapse in the first place. I wouldn't see her while she was intoxicated, but I called her on the mornings after she presented herself in my office like that. She fought hard to not listen as I explained that a warning was different than an invitation, and that she could maintain abstinence if she tried a different way. Her real problem was that she refused to find and use sources of support. Unfortunately, after several months, Tanya just stopped coming for treatment.

Eric, on the other hand, relapsed and dealt with it in a healthier way. Six months after I discharged him successfully, Eric returned to my office. He explained through his embarrassment that he had relapsed a month before. In that one month, everything about his addiction returned to the awful state of affairs that drove him into recovery in the first place: his wife was talking about divorce, he'd lost a contract he'd won as a private contractor, was messing up his current assignment so much he was going to lose money on the deal, and the night before had narrowly escaped from a police raid.

We discussed what had happened. Eric's plans of action were solid, and he'd followed them while he was in treatment. There was one unexpected event though; his friend David contacted him. David was the first name on Eric's high-risk characteristics list. Whenever Eric spent time with David, Eric used drugs.

What's important in this situation was that Eric was able to pinpoint exactly why his relapse occurred. There was nothing he couldn't figure out. When he described the situation, there was nothing vague in his report; he didn't try to rationalize or downplay the seriousness of it. More importantly, it was clear exactly where Eric's plan of action was flawed. Eric's plan gave great detail about how he'd avoid David at all costs. That part of the plan worked well. In five months, he made sure he never did anything that would allow him to contact David. He never planned out how he'd respond if David chose to contact him, however. His plan was not adequate in this regard. Unfortunately, neither Eric nor his support group nor I noticed this.

Eric and I revised his plan of action to become more precise in avoiding David. If David ever contacted Eric again, Eric would leave the situation immediately, no matter how important the situation he was in at the time (after all, if he hung around David, the situation would get bad enough in no time at all). Then, he would call his wife, sponsor, or any of five other sources of support, check in and make arrangements to have someone meet him shortly. In time, he hoped he wouldn't be bothered by David anymore. For now, he needed to revise his plan, jump back on the wagon, and continue with his abstinence. Don't forget this important fact: The more times you allow yourself to relapse, the less likely that you'll acquire permanent abstinence. It's important you stick with abstinence once you've started it. Don't get down on yourself if you do relapse, but make sure you increase your efforts to stay abstinent once you recover from your high.

You might take a lesson from the early recovery of the two founders of Alcoholics Anonymous and originators of the Twelve Steps. Both Bill Wilson and Bob Smith relapsed after they had already learned the importance of permanent lifestyle change. Both drank again while trying to maintain abstinence on their own. Bill drank again over the course of his first several days of trying to stay sober. Bob drank one more time for several days at the end of his first four weeks of sobriety. Bill and Bob stayed sober only after they met and began to help each other stay sober.

You can learn two lessons from this. First, relapse can happen in anyone's recovery, even the most legendary of recovering people, and even yours. Second, you have a better chance of recovery if you allow yourself to receive help from some of your sources of support. If you relapse, then contact one or more of them—pronto.

## Rely On Your Sources of Support

A returning theme in your recovery is that you should rely on sources of support besides yourself. Even though you're in charge of your recovery, your potential for relapse shrinks when you include others in your recovery plan. Remember, your best efforts by yourself didn't keep you abstinent. Interestingly, even critics of Twelve-Step programs acknowledge the need for outside support.

Critics of the Twelve Steps, even those who founded separate recovery programs, agree that recovery is more possible with outside support than alone. Sources of support help chemically dependent people do things beyond what they can do for themselves; like staying abstinent. Still, you might insist that things are different for you. Perhaps you feel that you don't need anything besides your own self-will. In the professional recovery field, this kind of stubbornness is called *terminal uniqueness*. That is, people who insist that the rules of recovery don't apply to them are bound for relapse.

Don't forget that there are people out there who know more about recovery than you do, and they're willing to give you a hand. When you've had enough of your own best efforts, then find some of those sources of support and take their advice.

# Short-Term Pain Equals Long-Term Gain

For chemically dependent people, using drugs or alcohol brings short-term gain, or instant gratification, but long-term pain. That means that as you approach the opportunity to use or drink, it can be exciting. When you actually do use or drink, it's enjoyable, and this is the short-term gain. Inevitably, the drugs or alcohol begin to wear off and you feel the remorse, the discouragement, the guilt, and the withdrawal symptoms. For chemically dependent people, this pain lasts longer than the thrill of using or drinking.

Recovery, especially the early days and weeks of recovery, brings you *short-term pain,* but *long-term gain*. The previous goals have involved difficult lifestyle changes, resulting insecurity, unfamiliar behaviors, and withdrawal symptoms all as a result of starting to recover. Early recovery is a lot to deal with—that is the short-term pain. However, you will also notice that the benefits from your abstinence feel better and better as your recovery continues—that is the *long-term gain.*

Your satisfaction, pride, sense of improvement and ability, improved relationships, job performance, debt improvements, improved legal status, and better health are all part of the long-term gain. You will enjoy the benefits as long as your abstinence and your recovery continue. This is your choice—you could make it continue for the rest of your life. Always remember to look back on how much you have accomplished in your recovery; you will feel rewarded and encouraged, especially in the face of how much work you may need to do still.

You will find it difficult to keep up the lifestyle changes necessary for recovery from chemical dependency at first. Imagine changing your religion, or your gender, or your culture. Imagine moving to a new country where you don't speak the language—

you would slowly learn the language, but it would take time. All of these changes have similarities to what it is like to change your chemical dependency lifestyle to your recovery lifestyle. Can you imagine doing any of those things easily? Could you really do any of them without some kind of help? The answer is no, which is another reason why you should not attempt recovery alone.

## Go for It—But Do It Right!

The process of recovery outlined in this book keeps you active and progressing from early, fragile attempts at abstinence, peppered with withdrawal symptoms, to longer-term and stable recovery with a healthy mind and body. Each goal builds on the others. With the right support, you can use this process to help you keep abstinent forever, even if there are other problems in your life that you're dealing with at the same time. All it takes is patience and perseverance on your part.

Recovery is your responsibility. Maintain your abstinence and you will feel the long-term benefits. Don't forget this will only happen as long as you rely on more than just your own best efforts to avoid relapse. But avoid relapse, and you'll improve your life. How much can you improve? Well, you'll be in charge of that.

After all, that's what you were wanting, right?

# 12

A Word to Therapists:
A Guide for Using
This Book in
Treatment Settings

If you are a therapist working with chemically dependent people, the ten therapeutic goals outlined in this book can be part of an effective treatment strategy. You can use these goals to formulate treatment plans, which can be valuable to a variety of counseling styles. This chapter is written to you, the therapist, as a guide on how to use these goals in your practice.

Treatment using these goals is highly structured, developmental, cognitive behavioral, and keeps patients active throughout their recovery process. These therapeutic goals have proven useful for therapists treating chemical dependency under models of therapy like psychology of mind, rational emotive therapy, neurolinquistic programming, rogerian, and gestalt. The process has worked with individual therapy, and is particularly effective with group therapy.

Professional chemical dependency therapy in combination with group support has more success for patients seeking recovery than nonprofessional group support. Still, patients who use these goals do so while maintaining their individuality. These goals can help your patients regardless of ethnicity, gender, culture, creed, socio-economic status, or personal beliefs. Each of your patients will develop a recovery plan that is different from the other patients. Help your patients complete goal work in order to develop a personalized plan of recovery that will work along with or despite their particular characteristics.

Your patients need to write down their goal work. They should do this on separate pieces of paper or in a journal. If a patient cannot write, then either arrange a way the patient can dictate or arrange for the patient to tape record the goals. This is important, as much of the goal work relies on previous goal work. Your patients will need to recall what they've already done. They shouldn't rely on their memories alone, and neither should you.

# Goal One: Diagnosing Your Patient

Therapy begins after you make an appropriate diagnosis. The process of recovery in this book is for chemical dependency; therefore for this process to work, you must make sure that your diagnosis of chemical dependency is accurate. If you try to treat something which isn't really there, you and your patients will not succeed.

For any treatment to work, your diagnosis establishing the need for treatment must be flawless. A diagnosis must be based on criteria, such as those established by the American Psychiatric Association or as established by the World Health Organization. A diagnosis must also be demonstrable and verifiable by other therapists who would use the same guidelines. Most importantly, a diagnosis must be understood by your patients before any kind of therapy will work to treat the chemical dependency.

Therapists sometimes make a diagnosis based on either too few criteria, or on the requirements of a third party such as a court official, an employer, or an angry relative of the patient. They may make a diagnosis more as a process of counter-transference than therapy—If I've got it, anyone in my office must have it, too. Diagnoses of addiction have also been made based upon nothing more than a patient's ability to pay for treatment. Not only are these faulty diagnostic techniques inaccurate, but they are also signs of inappropriate professional conduct. Furthermore, a patient who believes in a diagnosis based on these criteria has been brainwashed, not treated.

Make sure your diagnosis is accurate. Explain your diagnosis to your patients in language your patients can understand and accept. If they need simple terms, then use simple terms. Make sure they understand. If you do this, your patients will not argue about your diagnoses.

Additionally, remember that the process of therapy outlined in this book is for chemical dependency, not chemical abuse. These two disorders are different in that abuse *is not permanent*. Abuse is often a reaction to a stressor or influence in a patient's life. It may also indicate a pattern which would not be too hard for a patient to break if required to do so.

In any case, the treatment for abuse is less intense, less invasive, and less time-consuming than the treatment for chemical dependency. Patients treated for abuse shouldn't be in therapy with patients treating dependence. Their needs are different, and both will confuse the other when comparing symptoms, motivation, and the need for change. Use different education and change techniques to treat abuse. These therapeutic goals work best for dependence.

You can combine your therapeutic efforts at establishing a diagnosis with your patients' need to understand and make their own self-diagnosis. Fortunately, you both need to look for the same things. However, you will look for *diagnostic* signs and symptoms of chemical dependency, and your patients will look for signs and symptoms of *powerlessness* and *unmanageability*, as defined by the first goal. In the following sections, observe how these two efforts can blend. First you'll review powerlessness and unmanageability, followed by the criteria you need to adhere to from the *DSM-IV,* and by the World Health Organization, which appears in the *International Classification of Diseases and Behavioral Disorders: Diagnostic Criteria for Research.*

## Powerlessness, Unmanageability, and the Diagnostic Criteria

The criteria established by the American Psychiatric Association and printed in the *Diagnostic and Statistical Manual* (*Volume IV*) and by the World Health Organization (WHO) align with the concepts of your patients' first goal. Read about the process of your patients' self-diagnosis for further explanation.

### Powerlessness

Powerlessness means that when your patients choose to use drugs or drink alcohol, they cannot always predict how much they will consume. Powerlessness is usually demonstrated in the amount of drug or alcohol used, or in the amount of time or money spent when using or drinking. This characteristic aligns with *DSM* criteria and the WHO, which refer to tolerance, unpredictable consumption, and the inability to reduce or discontinue use.

### Unmanageability

Unmanageability means that when your patient uses drugs or alcohol, he or she cannot always predict what the consequences will be of his or her use. The *DSM-IV* and the WHO criteria that *do not* demonstrate your patient's powerlessness *do* demonstrate his or her unmanageability over use of drugs or alcohol. This includes not experiencing the same effect when using the same amount, withdrawal symptoms, lifestyle disruption, and continued use despite problems.

Unmanageability over the consequences of using drugs or alcohol is demonstrated under criterion one regarding tolerance. If a patient's body begins to react by developing tolerance to the extent that a *usual* amount of drugs or alcohol *produces a diminished effect*, that is a consequence of unmanageability. It would not have happened if the patient had not been using drugs or alcohol. For those same reasons, all the *withdrawal symptoms* listed in the criteria also demonstrate unmanageability.

Unmanageability is also demonstrated by the criterion that describes *spending more time to obtain drugs or alcohol*, or *recovering from an episode of using or drinking*. Nondependent drug or alcohol users do not face such a consequence, at least not routinely. If a patient can claim to have reduced or *given up important social, occupational*, or *recreational activities*, as in criterion six, that is a sign of unmanageability. If, as in another DSM and WHO criterion, a patient continues to use drugs or alcohol despite consequences that would tell a nondependent person to stop using or drinking, that too is a sign of unmanageability. In every case, these consequences probably wouldn't have happened if the patient had not used drugs or alcohol.

# A Developmental Model of Recovery

The original Twelve Steps created a guideline for a *developmental* process for recovery. That is, members of AA progress through a process, each step of which builds upon the work of the others already completed. Recovery develops over time by using those steps; it doesn't just occur like a cure such as an antidote for poisoning.

In 1986, Stephanie Brown published research in her book, *Treating the Alcoholic: A Developmental Model of Recovery*, on how eighty alcoholics developed their recovery by using the Twelve Steps. She found that their recovery occurred in four progressive developmental stages. Each stage had certain tasks that increased the AA member's awareness as to the nature of his or her condition. Also in each stage, a member grew to accept more responsibility to overcome the alcohol dependency, and became less reliant on outside influences to keep from relapsing. If a member avoided some of the tasks of one stage before beginning the work of another, the member relapsed.

Brown's research demonstrated a developmental approach to recovery, and provided the structure for a developmental model for treatment of all chemical dependencies, not just alcohol dependence. Other researchers have added to a growing body of information supporting the view that recovery does and should occur in phases. Brown identified four stages of recovery. All the subjects she researched began recovery in a *use* stage, wherein the alcoholics actively abused alcohol and denied they had a problem. Recovery continued through *transition* and *early recovery* phases, ending with *ongoing recovery*.

The process of recovery in this book presents a developmental model for treatment and recovery. When followed appropriately, this model can guide patients from the *use phase* (the phase at which most patients enter therapy) through *ongoing recovery* (where optimally, patients should receive a discharge).

What follows is a more thorough description of Brown's developmental stages of recovery combined with the therapeutic goals of treatment. The goals and phases have been aligned with each other. Each goal includes some therapeutic notes and instructions offering suggestions on the best way you can use this process in your practice. Each of these goals is more thoroughly explained, from the patient's point of view, in the earlier chapters of this book. Each goal is presented as the therapeutic goal of your treatment plan. In the simplest form, this process is a ten-goal course of therapy to help chemically dependent patients work through the developmental phases of recovery.

## Use Phase

At this phase, chemically dependent people only want to continue their drug or alcohol use. They maintain a lifestyle and a mind-set supporting their drinking or drug use. They utilize a denial system helping to justify their use as perfectly natural and part of otherwise unremarkable lives. They have no interest in pursuing any therapy that would include abstinence. Trying to provide therapy is impractical at this time. Professional intervention is limited to crisis management, crisis resolution, or other therapeutic services prior to beginning treatment.

Before they begin treatment, you can counsel your patients to work on overcoming their resistance. This isn't one of the therapeutic goals, but it is often a necessity before treatment can begin. A patient who wants only to maintain the option of using drugs or alcohol will not succeed in treatment that is designed to facilitate abstinence. You could guide these patients through an honest evaluation of their use or drinking apart from those services designed to promote abstinence. You could use a format identical to the work of the first therapeutic goal—helping patients identify the symptoms and consequences of drug or alcohol use toward making a self-diagnosis. Most patients will not make a commitment to pursue this kind of counseling without some kind of external motivation prompting them to consider change, such as the threat of certain legal, occupational, or relationship consequences. When possible, work with the coercive third parties in your patients' lives to help motivate them to work. If they can overcome their resistance, then proceed with this process. If not, then discharge them from your service, and allow them to deal with the third parties. It may be that your patients decide to come back for your therapy in their futures.

Once a patient has realized he or she has some kind of problem with drugs or alcohol, treatment can begin. At the start of this process, the patient enters the transition phase of recovery.

## Transition Phase

This phase begins when chemically dependent people realize that they have indeed caused problems in their lives because of their use of drugs or alcohol. They realize this after some attention-getting situation that makes them realize they would not have suffered the problem if they had not used or drank. Only now will chemically dependent people begin to consider identifying themselves as chemically dependent. Under therapeutic circumstances, they will accept this with a self-diagnosis. They begin to identify with other people recovering from similar problems. Patients also begin to accept their responsibilities for recovery.

However, their acceptance is fragile. They can easily backtrack, and again deny that their drug or alcohol use is as truly problematic as others believe. This will happen when the chemically dependent person doesn't have enough encouragement or support for maintaining abstinence or developing an abstinence-based lifestyle. The following goals can help a patient through the transition phase of recovery:

**Goal 1:** *The patient makes a self-diagnosis of chemical dependency.* No one will treat what they don't believe they have. With this goal, you teach your patients about chemical dependency. Explain the concepts of *powerlessness* and *unmanageability,* and that these symptoms are permanent when you have chemical dependency. Then help your patients identify whatever symptoms they have. Have them record these somehow, preferably in a notebook or in a journal. They should identify at least ten symptoms as examples of powerlessness and ten symptoms as examples of unmanageability. Based on the symptoms they identify, and the permanent nature of the symptoms, help them understand why these mean they have chemical dependency. Help them clarify this in a self-diagnosis. Have your patient record their self-diagnosis also.

**Goal 2:** *The patient identifies sources of support that will help them overcome the chemical dependency.* Help your patients understand that they must work toward abstinence as the primary objective of recovery. This is how they can get sound judgment back in their lives. Teach your patients that they must have outside support in order to maintain their abstinence. If your patients object to this, then help them remember their failed attempts at trying to remain abstinent all by themselves.

Your patients should identify at least ten people and things that could help them maintain abstinence. At least half of those sources need to be living, accessible human beings. Help them record these on a list. Discuss their lists with them, and have them discuss their lists with the members of the therapeutic community who attend treatment with them. Make sure the sources of support they identify will help them maintain abstinence. Your patients will use these sources of support throughout the rest of treatment.

**Goal 3:** *The patient makes a commitment to work.* Discuss how recovery can happen in general terms with your patients. They should express some willingness to follow the guidance of those sources of support in order to avoid relapse and maintain abstinence. Consider having your patients demonstrate this willingness. For example, they could present signatures on a support-group attendance-verification record, or a phone list demonstrating participation in some kind of a support group. When patients indicate that they can make such a commitment, they complete this goal.

## Early Recovery Phase

In this phase, chemically dependent people have a stronger identification as having chemical dependency. They also have a strong commitment to maintain their abstinence. They realize that their chemical use has created some kind of problem in most areas of their lives, not just one or a few. Their focus moves away from merely staying away from drugs and alcohol. They begin to create a lifestyle based on remaining permanently abstinent. They accept a lot of external direction while creating this new lifestyle.

At this stage, recovering people become aware of their feelings again. They may feel vulnerable and uncomfortable, and they usually feel depressed. If the patient refuses to acknowledge that important events have had some emotional impact, the patient becomes at risk for relapse again.

**Goal 4:** *The patient makes a lifestyle inventory and discusses it.* Now you help your patients figure out what in their lifestyles allows for relapse (high-risk thoughts, attitudes, and behaviors) and what in their lifestyles already supports abstinence (low-risk thoughts, attitudes, and behaviors). Help your patients create two lists.

They should record at least twenty specific thoughts, attitudes, and behaviors as examples of high-risk lifestyle characteristics, and another twenty examples of low-risk characteristics. Your patients should discuss those lists with you, with some of their other sources of support, and with the therapeutic community. The feedback your patients receive will help them understand the nature of their lifestyle leading to either relapse or abstinence. This discussion will also help your patients identify thoughts, attitudes, and behaviors they might have overlooked.

**Goal 5:** *The patient makes a commitment to lifestyle change.* Discuss with your patients the need for lifestyle changes. The first part of that change will remove their opportunities to engage in high-risk thoughts, attitudes, and behaviors. The second part will increase and enhance their low-risk thoughts, attitudes, and behaviors.

If you have been conducting these goals in a group setting, take time now to discuss the commitment of each patient in an individual session. The session probably won't need to last more than a half-hour. When your patients express a willingness to change, and a desire to know how to make these lifestyle changes, then they have completed this goal.

**Goal 6:** *The patient develops a plan of action to avoid relapse and to remain abstinent.* Have your patients develop a two-part personalized plan of action. One part is a plan to reduce their potential for relapse. The other part is to improve their likelihood to remain abstinent. Your patients base this plan on their lists of high-risk and low-risk thoughts, attitudes, and behaviors which they developed with the fourth goal.

They should create a plan removing the influence of each high-risk thought, attitude, and behavior they identified. They also write a plan reinforcing each low-risk thought, attitude, and behavior. As part of the plan, your patients should include how they will use their sources of support they identified with the second goal. To get feedback and to help themselves troubleshoot, they should discuss this plan of action with their therapeutic community.

**Goal 7:** *The patient puts that plan of action to work.* Now your patients begin to live by their plan of action. The only restriction is if a part of their plan proves to actually threaten their recovery or hurt someone more than it would help them. Make sure they discuss their perceptions of success or problems with the therapeutic community.

## Ongoing Recovery Phase

At this phase recovering people have a strong personal commitment and internal motivation to remain abstinent. Patients choose to pursue abstinence regardless of outside events. They have adopted whatever personal recovery plan they developed as a solid part of their lifestyles. They avoid high-risk situations and behaviors as a matter of course, and think and behave in low-risk ways without needing a reminder to do so. This commitment might be so ingrained that an observer may not be able to notice that the patient is living by any particular plan that supports the abstinence.

Recovering people may not need attend as many support groups or as much professional therapy now as in the transition or early phases of recovery. Nonetheless, they maintain their abstinence. They respect the need to remain abstinent in all they do, and thereby pursue recovery in all aspects of their lives.

They become aware of secondary recovery issues and can deal with them appropriately while still maintaining abstinence. Patients tackle more and more personal challenges and do not let those challenges affect their abstinence. Your patients' lifestyles could be as healthy and no more involved than that of any other patient who works on improving their lifestyle.

**Goal 8:** *The patient evaluates how the plan is working, and makes appropriate changes when necessary.* As long as the plan works to keep them abstinent, patients acknowledge their time in recovery with some modest personal praise. When the plan proves inadequate to help a patient deal with something in his or her life, then that patient revises the plan to make it more effective. These changes should be made with your guidance and the therapeutic community's feedback. Even though the plan can change, the purpose of any revision in the plan still serves to protect abstinence.

**Goal 9:** *The patient identifies new sources of support for new problems that require more or different modes of support.* If patients realize that the sources of support they identified with the second goal are inadequate to help resolve a new problem, then they identify new sources of support. These could be anyone or anything, just as long as the patients can use the new source. The only restriction to selecting a new source of support is that new sources must respect the patients' need to maintain abstinence. After identifying the new sources of support, patients use them to overcome the new problems.

**Goal 10:** *The patient, having demonstrated ability to maintain abstinence, pursues recovery in all aspects of life.* This serves as a therapeutic declaration that your patients have internalized the responsibility for recovery. Therapist and patients agree that the patients have demonstrated the ability to maintain abstinence regardless of what circumstances might occur in their lives.

# Therapeutic Process

The therapeutic process has proven effective in a variety of treatment venues. Here are some suggestions for using these therapeutic goals in different courses of treatment. These are suggestions that have worked for actual treatment programs which use this model:

## Outpatient Treatment

You can use these goals in a therapeutic process for outpatient chemical dependency treatment. The program allows individualized-treatment planning for all patients. A program, for example, could begin three nights each week, and end with once-a-week participation. Depending on the motivation and the abilities of the patients, participation at the intensive outpatient level varies from between twenty to thirty-five sessions, before weekly aftercare.

Under the best circumstances, you could divide the program into four levels of treatment. Each level is conducted as a group separate from the other levels.

All patients begin at level one. This level should not be open-ended; that is, new patients should not arrive every day the group is held. Begin new patients on the same day of each week. Newcomers wait to begin treatment until the next start-day, then join the others already in level one. After that, patients advance through each level at their own pace. Do not delay patients' movement from level to level. Allow them to move from level one to two, two to three and three to four when appropriate, and let them join patients who advanced before them.

Make sure your patients have some kind of orientation prior to the first session of level one. Teach your patients five ground rules: (1) protect the confidentiality of other members, (2) no alcohol or drug use, (3) be on time, (4) attend outside recovery support groups, and (5) pay whatever payment they are required to make, if any.

All these ground rules should be requirements for an approved discharge. Any violation of these ground rules should be grounds for administrative discharge from the program. This is also the time to teach the requirements around any random urine drug-screening that you conduct, optimally at the first session.

This process works particularly well in a group format. An effective group format allows each patient to present completed goal-work in a written format for the other patients in the group to see, such as on a chalkboard. Each patient, in turn, explains each element of the goal-work and asks for feedback. Your patients can give and receive feedback and, most importantly, call each other on suspicious or nontherapeutic work. Addicts in new recovery are more adept, at times, than seasoned therapists when it comes to calling each other on their resistance, deception, or denial. The result for your patients is more accurate goal-work, and a positive group experience that they can carry into a nonprofessional support group. The result for you is that you can spend more time facilitating a successful group, rather than dealing with group dynamics that are focused on resistance and denial.

**Level I:** In level one, patients complete goals one, two, and three. Therapists act as facilitators: they teach as well as counsel. Teach your patients the fundamentals behind the first two goals. Give them the four homework assignments and help them complete them. More tenured patients should help teach and challenge the newer patients.

When patients demonstrate a thorough understanding of their diagnosis and the need to continue with treatment, they complete the third goal. At this point they move on to level two. Most patients will finish level one in six sessions.

**Level II:** Level two covers goals four and five. The group discusses the identified thoughts, attitudes, and behaviors with each other.

Be aware of reports that sound suspicious, such as reports in which the patient downplays the severity of a situation, or incredible reports which sound more like bragging.

Teach your patients about their need for commitment to change. Give them at least one night to really think about these changes before conducting the individual session to complete the fifth goal. In that session, the patient should express a desire to continue with treatment and ask to learn how. When this happens, move your patient on to level three. Patients should finish level two in around seven sessions.

**Level III:** Level three comprises goals six, seven, eight, and nine. Each session, patients either work on creating their plan of action, or they give updates on their plans' effectiveness. All patients participate in this discussion. This gives each patient the opportunity to consider his or her own plan of recovery in the light of another patient's plan.

At least once a week, some unexpected occurrence inevitably will challenge one of your patients' recovery. When it happens, explain the eighth goal to your patients. Let the group discuss the goal in terms of resolving the particular challenge the patient has brought up. Let everyone see how the patient can modify the plan of action successfully. Make sure he or she returns with reports about the effectiveness of the modifications. Each patient will get frequent reminders on how to use the eighth goal in their own lives. They will have the opportunity to demonstrate this knowledge when similar problems arise in their own recovery.

When especially challenging problems arise, you should explain the ninth goal. Your patients will then make more significant modifications in their plans, including identifying and using new sources of support. When it's appropriate, make a referral to another therapeutic source. You could even set up a resource list for your patients to use to learn who or what could help them overcome the most frequently raised new problems.

You should not graduate your patients from level three until you believe they demonstrate an ability and a conviction to maintain recovery in any life circumstance. Typically, their participation in level three will last at least twelve sessions, and usually longer.

**Level IV:** Level four can be a weekly, low-intensive follow-up to level three. Level four begins the transition away from constant professional monitoring of the patient. Patients attend a session a week for as long as it takes for you, as a therapist, to feel comfortable they can continue abstinence and relapse prevention without the structure of your group. However, this may not take more than twelve sessions.

Your patients can describe the success of their programs of recovery, and give each other encouragement and praise. They can also discuss the challenges to their programs, seeking advice and accepting feedback on how they are already handling those challenges.

Teach the concepts behind the tenth goal, and help them to learn that their recovery is a permanent responsibility. Discharge your patients when they demonstrate an internalized desire to maintain their abstinence and an ability to do so. They will probably not have moved fully into the ongoing recovery phase, but will have an exceptional chance of doing so if they have abided by the goals.

## *Inpatient or Residential Treatment*

In a residential setting, it is impractical to segregate patients by levels. That would require separate residential units for each level of treatment described in the outline for outpatient program. That is unnecessary.

Healthier and longer tenured members of a therapeutic community can have a beneficial and therapeutic effect on newer members. The seasoned members can show how a commitment to long-lasting abstinence helps their maturity, disposition, decision-making abilities, attitude, outlook on life, and emotional state. These members can also provide therapeutic peer support for newer members still ambivalent about treatment and recovery. Learning by example is a benefit to a residential setting that a therapist just cannot offer by him- or herself.

The environment of a residential setting, however, differs from the environment of an outpatient therapy group. Usually, patients in residential settings have had more problems with their drug or alcohol use than patients in outpatient settings. Also, these patients come from poor environments that wouldn't support the changes necessary for recovery. Residential treatment can also include more repetitious, and even more aggressive therapy than the less frequent setting of outpatient treatment.

A wise approach to residential treatment using the goals would be to separate the newest patients from the longer-tenured patients when they participate in therapy groups. In this way, the new patients won't be overwhelmed by the more intensive work done by more tenured patients. The "old-timers" won't be bored watching the new patients work through denial. Still, the more seasoned patients can influence the newer ones in the treatment setting outside of therapy groups.

Consider separating the patients during therapy groups at least until after the newer patients complete the third goal. Consider placing those patients in an *orientation group* focusing on the first three goals.

When they join the other members, the newer patients can introduce themselves to the larger group by reading their self-diagnosis. They can explain the work they have completed thus far to identify symptoms of their dependency and sources of support. This therapeutic presentation gives every member of the therapeutic community a clear understanding of everyone else, and helps the process of therapeutic bonding.

Patients in a residential setting could complete the first three goals quickly—perhaps in a matter of a few days. This assumes that patients have begun treatment after necessary detoxification, and after any necessary crisis resolution.

If, however, after a week in residential treatment the patient has been unable to make a self-diagnosis and commit to further treatment, then the patient may indeed be unable to progress at all. One of these things has happened: either (1) the patient doesn't really have chemical dependency, or (2) has suffered drug-induced brain damage so extensively that this cognitive approach proves inappropriate for their needs, or (3) the patient is so resistant to the idea of therapy that he or she chooses to participate minimally and passively.

If the patient doesn't have chemical dependency, the patient should receive a discharge to a reduced level of treatment. If the patient needs an evaluation for brain damage or mental impairment, then arrange such an evaluation. Unless your program has the capability to care for such patients, this kind of patient may need to discontinue treatment until after the impairment is resolved.

In the third condition, you may need to develop additional therapeutic goals to identify and overcome the resistance. Perhaps they can develop a concurrent plan of action or goal to overcome their reluctance to therapy. Work out a plan to help determine what it would take for them to become more committed. How could they succeed at developing their commitment? With whom should they discuss their motivation?

However, if it becomes clear that the patient cannot succeed using this therapeutic process, then discharge the patient. Discharge the patient to another setting that can deal with the patient's problem, or just discharge the patient with an invitation to return after he or she makes a firmer commitment to treatment.

Any patient in residential treatment should be able to finish the first six therapeutic goals in under three weeks. From then on, their work focuses on the last four goals, which implement, evaluate, and add to their plan of action.

You can introduce new therapeutic issues while your patients work on these last four goals. Depending on the length of the program, your patients could make impressive strides toward settling emotional issues such as establishing healthier relationships, developing a healthier self-esteem, or grieving the loss of an important relationship. They could also begin work toward resolving more involved personal issues.

Remember, however, that you and your patients shouldn't explore intense emotional issues this early in the patient's recovery. You shouldn't try and treat issues like incest or child molestation, child abuse, or the results of an abusive family of origin yet. These issues shouldn't be addressed until after many months and perhaps years of abstinence.

## Multiple Levels of Treatment

With the advent of managed care and the rising tide of research in the field of treatment, many programs have found unexpected success with differing therapeutic levels of treatment. Some

programs treat chemical dependency by utilizing an initial residential setting, followed by some partial-hospitalization or day-
treatment participation, continued with outpatient treatment several days each week, and ending with months-long participation
of weekly aftercare.

Again, the therapeutic goals in this book are compatible.
Adapt the levels of treatment outlined in the previous outpatient
treatment section. Goals one, two, and three could be the primary
goals of a residential setting. Goals four and five could be the focus of partial-hospitalization or day treatment, and the patient
could begin goal six. Goals six, seven, eight, and nine could be the
focus of outpatient treatment. Aftercare could comprise goal ten.

## Individual Therapy

These goals also work with patients who cannot participate
in a group process for treatment. Assign your patients the work
on these goals in order, one goal at a time. Sometimes the work
for a goal, like goals three and five, is completed within the scope
of one individual session. Other goals, particularly those requiring
"homework" like goals one, two, four, eight, and nine, will take
two to several sessions. The time your patient will need to work
through these goals will be quicker than in a group process. Hopefully, you can arrange therapy sessions with little time between
sessions.

An individual process will probably take less time than a
group process to get to the sixth goal. For the first five goals,
you'll spend a lot of time in session explaining this therapeutic
process, and helping the patient understand how to apply the goal
to his or her life and recovery. Thereafter, the focus of therapy is
on developing and strengthening the plan of action. Now the patient should spend more time than you talking about the goals
and recovery.

Plan to spend many sessions discussing the patient's success
at overcoming challenges. When appropriate, introduce the goals
helping the patient understand how to overcome secondary recovery issues raised in the course of the seventh, eighth, and ninth
goals. Again, make sure you have resources to which you can refer your patients when their issues are beyond your scope of practice or ability.

## *Low-Intensive or Education Services*

Within the scope of low-intensity, pretreatment, preliminary or education services, these goals and their concepts can prove beneficial to your work. The concepts of the first goal specifically help explain the dynamics of chemical dependency to your patients. Also, the nonspiritual focus of the therapeutic goals help explain the concepts of Twelve-Step programs.

Patients who resist considering whether or not they have symptoms of chemical dependency will often be more willing to explore whether or not they have signs of powerlessness or unmanageability, as defined by these therapeutic goals. Patients could diagnose themselves without even realizing they have done so! Of course, this requires careful therapeutic processing on your part, lest your patients accuse you of trickery.

Patients who hesitate to attend Twelve-Step meetings because of rumors or their own misunderstandings of the program may become willing to attend once they understand a nonspiritual explanation of recovery that parallels the steps.

Consider using the goals in your education program. Use the concepts that work best for short-term understanding. Consider especially the concepts found in the first, third, and sixth, and seventh goals.

# The Therapeutic Goals and ASAM Criteria

Among the administrative challenges facing therapists is the requirement to demonstrate a clinical need for treatment, and then the effectiveness of treatment provided to patients. The patients themselves may want this proof, but so do third-party payers and administrative bodies overseeing the performance of an individual therapist or the effectiveness of a clinic.

Partly in response to this, the American Society of Addiction Medicine (ASAM) has established patient placement and continued service criteria for the variety of possible substance-abuse services. Not diagnostic criteria, these are designed to offer a guideline to therapists to help determine what circumstances and symptoms warrant particular levels of care, including detoxification, and justification for continued services after that care has begun.

ASAM criteria comprise six dimensions of therapeutic concern. These dimensions help establish a patient's needs for treatment. When a patient has therapeutic problems in one or more dimensions, therapists and treatment programs can make decisions regarding what level of service the patient should pursue (like education, low-intensive outpatient, intensive outpatient, day treatment/partial hospitalization, or residential services).

A patient need not demonstrate significant therapeutic need in all six dimensions at all times. The dimensions are designed to allow therapists to demonstrate a need for treatment in order to address a patient's needs in any dimension. During the course of therapy, problems identified as being part of any particular dimension should resolve. If not, this would demonstrate the need to change the treatment plan. It could also demonstrate the need for a more intensive level of treatment. Also, in the course of treatment problems falling under the categories of other dimensions could become evident, requiring the need for changes in treatment plans, new treatment plans, or different levels of treatment.

Additionally, you can get an idea as to what goals the patient should pursue in order to overcome any deficits indicated by a particular dimension. As the patient makes therapeutic improvements, ASAM criteria help guide the therapist into deciding whether or not the patient can move to another, less-restrictive level of care; say, from day treatment to outpatient to aftercare services.

ASAM criteria have developed over the past few years into a credible and helpful tool for therapists. Whether or not you formally use ASAM criteria in your practice, you should be familiar with the ASAM guidelines, as they promote good treatment.

What follows are the dimensions established by ASAM and a brief synopsis of the dimension. (For a more thorough and complete understanding of the criteria, read the ASAM manual *The ASAM Patient Placement Criteria, Second Edition.*) Additionally, following the synopsis is an explanation as to which of the therapeutic goals of the process in this book could help address the therapeutic needs of a patient having trouble in the dimension.

**Dimension 1:** *Acute Intoxication and/or Withdrawal Potential* This dimension primarily helps determine whether or not a patient should pursue detoxification services or acute services designed to help a patient avoid injury during the course of withdrawal. In this dimension, these therapeutic goals may serve little purpose. The therapeutic goals are designed to be goals for treatment, and will not directly help a patient needing detox services.

However, the first three goals could be used as part of the education provided to a patient who is undergoing inpatient detoxification services.

If the patient is pursuing outpatient or ambulatory detox services, then the patient could begin treatment while in those services.

**Dimension 2:** *Biomedical Conditions and Complications* This dimension helps determine if secondary medical or health conditions, besides withdrawal, would complicate treatment and recovery.

If a patient has a medical condition which complicates treatment, goals four through nine can help handle the patient's needs. With goal four, the patient can identify how that condition complicates abstinence, or encourages relapse. The plan of action in goal six can address the need to care for the condition while maintaining abstinence. The next goals can help the patient, and you, monitor the success or short-fall of the plan. If a medical condition becomes evident after goal six is completed, use the new diagnosis as part of goals eight or nine.

**Dimension 3:** *Emotional/Behavioral Conditions and Complications* This dimension is similar to dimension two, in that it helps identify a secondary issue which could complicate treatment and recovery. This dimension, however, deals with emotional, psychiatric, or personality disorders. Again, goals four through nine could address these issues.

At goal four, the patient should identify high-risk and low-risk thoughts, attitudes, and behaviors for both chemical dependency as well as the mental illness. The remaining goals should address both issues as part of planning for relapse-prevention and abstinence-protection.

**Dimension 4:** *Treatment Acceptance/Resistance* The title says it all: this dimension helps evaluate the patients buy-in to the need for treatment. Here, goals one through three, five, and seven will help overcome resistance to treatment and help the patient accept the need for ongoing recovery.

**Dimension 5:** *Relapse/Continued Use Potential* Effective treatment should reduce the significance of this dimension as treatment continues. Any of the goals could address problems covered under this dimension.

Goals one through seven can address a patient's potential for relapse or continued use during the patient's earliest and most vulnerable days of abstinence.

Once the lifestyle plan is put into place, with the seventh goal, the patient's commitment to abstinence should be more evident. The next goals can help the patient examine the commitment while evaluating the plan of action.

**Dimension 6:** *Recovery Environment* This dimension addresses problems with a patient's community of residence or home environment. If a patient's living situation would make abstinence difficult, the therapist should be able to determine this during the therapeutic discussions necessary with the third and fifth goals; then the matter becomes an issue for later goal-work.

# Therapeutic Goals and Your Treatment Style

Tailor this process to your own therapeutic style. This book offers a format, not a list of commandments. If you use these goals and their vocabulary, and follow the general guidelines throughout this book, this approach will work for you, regardless of the kind of therapy or treatment modality you provide.

However, if you try and adapt this approach to a therapeutic style that hasn't worked for you before, don't expect this approach to fix your problems. This approach cannot do damage control for nontherapeutic treatment styles. If you need to, seek additional training before continuing to provide chemical dependency treatment to people needing skilled care.

# A Few Notes on this Treatment Process

Here are some final tips for you to get the most out of these goals in your practice.

## Managed Care and This Process

A therapist shouldn't rush patients into a new goal or a new level of therapy just because they seem to be taking too long.

Optimally, patients should receive a therapeutic discharge only after they have reached the *tenth goal* of treatment. This will concern therapists and programs working with a tradition dictating that treatment must last a specific amount of time. These goals represent a process for therapy, not for certain time frames. Patients treated under this model are not abusing the process by remaining in one level or with one goal for too long.

Therapists and programs dealing with the constraints of managed care may also worry that third party payers will refuse appropriate lengths of stay. These goals help you plan a clear-cut, developmental process for recovery that complies with ASAM criteria. This program provides a verifiable process, and will help you demonstrate clear progress when asking those providers for extensions for patients. You should be able to explain the problems a patient is having with a particular goal and the third parties will understand what you mean.

## Twelve-Step Programs and the Therapeutic Process

Patients will be able to see the similarity between this therapy process and the spiritual program outlined by the Twelve Steps. In most cases, patients will have no trouble using Twelve-Step programs along with these goals. Since patients should attend some kind of nonprofessional group support, and AA and NA are the most available support groups for chemical dependency, there is a good chance your patients will attend Twelve-Step groups.

However, you should warn you patients (perhaps often) that they shouldn't try to convince members of Twelve-Step programs that their use of the steps are wrong, and that the patients have a keener insight into recovery because of this process. Some individuals in Twelve-Step groups will criticize these goals, and the patients who attend treatment using these goals. Counsel your patients to look beyond these personalities-before-principles conflicts when they occur. When necessary, advise your patients to avoid certain meetings whose membership has shown hostility to this therapeutic program.

These goals don't threaten the stability of AA, NA, Women for Sobriety, Rational Recovery, or Secular Organizations for

Sobriety, incidentally. These groups are free-standing, nonprofessional support groups, which have helped people stay clean and sober longer than this therapeutic style.

# Secondary Recovery Issues Should Wait

The recommendation to avoid exploring emotional issues until later in recovery comes from a combination of practical experience and the results of many researchers in this field. When a patient focuses on an emotionally intense secondary recovery issue, the patient pays attention to little else. When this happens too early in the process of chemical dependency recovery, the patient loses the focus necessary to succeed through the early recovery phase. That is, the patient self-identifies not as a chemically dependent person, but as someone only with a complicated emotional issue that makes them drink too much alcohol or use drugs.

During the transition and early recovery phases, patients often maintain ambivalence toward their commitment for recovery. They are still apt to blame their relapses on other influences and deny that their dependency really exists. That ambivalence, plus an early-recovering dependent person's ever present tendency to want to focus on something other than recovery, is a nontherapeutic combination.

Patients who are encouraged by a professional to delve into an exploration of their complex emotional life and avoid focus on their dependency will probably not succeed in treatment. They will use their denial system to justify leaving treatment to go pursue the resolution of those other issues.

Then they'll probably use those issues to justify returning to drink or use, again. "After all," they will reason, "facing up to that stuff is tough and I need some relief. Besides, I really don't have chemical dependency, I've just got this nagging issue to contend with."

Therapists sometimes have trouble tempering their energy with a particularly troubled patient. Chemical dependency therapy is demanding and often unrewarding. The seductive potential of encouraging a patient to discuss something other than the dependency is sometimes too enticing to avoid.

Some therapists base their success as a therapist on the emotional outbursts of their patients. For example, a patient might resist discussing dependency, but become tearful when the therapist encourages discussion about the patient's family of origin. Taking the bait, the therapist focuses the patient's attention on the family history, not on recovery. A lot of emotional ventilation and catharsis occurs, but little real therapy for chemical dependency treatment. A managed-care organization would be within its rights to deny coverage for this kind of therapy done in the name of chemical dependency treatment.

Do not encourage your patients to explore secondary recovery issues too early in therapy. You do not need to forbid them from raising the issues; but when they do, acknowledge their issue and guide them back to the work of the particular therapeutic goal they're working on in this process. Let them know that they'll have opportunities to discuss those issues in the future, when they work on the later goals.

## Be Selective and Sensitive When Refusing to Discuss Secondary Recovery Issues

Some therapists have taken this counsel to the extreme. They assume that the recommendation to delay therapy on secondary recovery issues means that nothing besides chemical dependency should ever be discussed in treatment. This is not the case. Throughout treatment, it may be appropriate to offer some education or some skills-building classes.

However, education is not therapy by itself. Education makes patients aware of an issue, and how to view the issue in a healthy way. Such issues include explanations about how the body reacts to certain drugs, what the patient can expect in terms of drug interactions, cross-dependency, and cross-tolerance. Education could help patients learn abstinence-protecting alternatives to the treatment of future illnesses. Education could teach patients the importance of proper diet, sleep, exercise, group support, companionship, and socializing to help them maintain abstinence.

Likewise, skills-building alone is not therapy. However, skills-building could teach how to accomplish a task in a healthy way that supports recovery. This could include experiential classes in effective parenting, diet planning, financial planning, personal hygiene, and relaxation techniques. It could also include teaching job skills or getting through the maze of social service systems in your area. Skills-building might even include experiences designed to help a person learn to socialize and get along with people in healthier ways.

Of course, anything learned by a patient under the guise of education or skills-building could still raise emotional issues for the patient. Education and skills-building efforts should not aim to create such emotional release, however.

Nonetheless, careful planning and cautions by staff at a treatment program may still not thwart certain patients from reacting to presentations in emotional ways. When this happens, deal with the result as you would a crisis management issue. Allow the patient to discuss the issue. If necessary, have the patient do this alone or at least away from patients likely to feed into or off of such catharsis. Acknowledge the issue and the patient's feelings. Then, as appropriate, counsel the patient to hold off on further exploration and resolution of the issue until later on in the therapeutic process. Give the patient an idea of when that might be.

When necessary, provide crisis intervention or emergency services for the patient. These services, of course, would supersede the treatment goals in this book.

## Discharge Criteria

There are two reasons to discharge a patient from this process. The first reason is when your patient has *successfully* and *appropriately* completed all the work on these goals. This means that your patient demonstrates consistent willingness and ability to comply with the altered plan of action; and your patient also demonstrates ability to react to situations by protecting his or her abstinence without needing to check with you or the treatment group first.

In this situation, you can discharge your patient from further treatment. If it's possible and practical, allow the patient to participate in aftercare whenever the patient would want to return. Make sure your patient knows other sources of therapy or professional support. Allow them to feel welcome to return to your services.

The second reason for discharge is when it becomes obvious to you, your staff, or a treatment team that further treatment *will not* help the patient. In this situation, the patient will not have completed all goals of treatment. Usually, the patient will have gotten stuck on one goal for a while.

The patient in this situation demonstrates little interest in treatment. If the patient doesn't drop out, he or she might attend only to satisfy a court or state agency that has mandated a successful completion. The patient may be argumentative, will probably belittle the efforts of others in treatment, may frequently test positive on urine analyses, or report frequent relapses.

If patient begins this nontherapeutic behavior, you should adapt your style and these goals to try and resolve the problem. You might consider an abstinence contract, with the result of violation being a more intensive level of treatment.

You might consider removing the patient from the group process. Handle things in individual therapy until the patient can return with more commitment.

You can explore other issues which may occur in your patient's life that she or he reacts to as though they were crises. In that case, allow the patient to leave treatment to engage in crisis management until the patient can commit to the recovery process again.

However, if all efforts to improve a patient's motivation to change meet with failure, then discharge your patient. Your patient will have demonstrated a firm unwillingness to participate in your program. This is certainly the patient's right. You shouldn't feel obligated to risk compromising your program and the therapy of other patients by holding on to a resistant patient in the hopes that things will get better. If your patient has to deal with the consequences of a third party like a court or state agency, then perhaps that third party will help motivate the patient in the future.

Discharge the patient with an invitation to return after certain circumstances are met. Unless the patient has done something illegal in your agency, give them the feeling that you would welcome them back and treat them fairly if they make the choice to pursue treatment on your terms. However, require that the patient stay away from treatment for some specified length of time prior to a reevaluation and reconsideration for admission.

# The Therapeutic Approach to Chemical Dependency

This process works for therapists as well as patients. It provides a concise, verifiable, goal-oriented, and developmental approach to chemical dependency treatment. Therapists find the process—particularly the first goal—a helpful part of helping their patients find recovery. The process will work for you and your patients too. Good luck as you determine how best to use the goals and the process in your practice.

# 13

## Resources for Support

Here are some final tips on finding sources of support to help your recovery.

## Finding a Support Group or a Professional

**Ask around.** You could ask anyone who is already helping you if they've seen a group or a professional advertised to help further with your problem. Advertisements or announcements for groups might be printed in your newspaper's community calendar, in a local magazine, in a church bulletin, or on TV or the radio in the form of a public service announcement. Professionals serving people in recovery will often advertise in the same places, though you may find their advertisements more often in a newspaper or magazine than TV or the radio.

You may know somebody who has overcome the problem affecting you. Ask them or their friends if they found a group that was helpful. Did they hire the services of a professional? Did they like that professional? If they did, then get the name of who they worked with.

**Use the Phone Book.** Try the Yellow Pages under certain headings. For example, you may find a recovery support group under drug abuse treatment. A professional might be found there also, as well as under the headings mental health services, or therapists. You could always call directory assistance for help.

**Call a Pro.** If a support group meets in your area, then someone has its meeting time and day on a list. Call the professionals in your area who would most likely know. Try your local mental health center, a psychiatric clinic, a treatment center, or a community services referral agency. While you're on the phone, you might want to make an appointment for yourself to go in and see someone.

**Find a Referral Source.** Many communities have organizations that give the names of professional and nonprofessional organizations that can help your recovery. These agencies can usually give you the information over the phone. Check your phone book for the listing of a community referral center. Sometimes, you'll find them listed on the inside front cover of your phone book. Again, if you can't find the number in the phone book, there's always directory assistance.

A few national organizations give information on a surprising number of different support groups and organizations. An excellent resource is the American Self-Help Clearinghouse. This organization publishes *The Self-Help Sourcebook*, which lists several hundred self-help groups and organizations categorized according to the problem each group addresses. It also lists referral agencies, toll-free numbers, clearinghouses, and other resources, nationally and by state. It provides ideas for starting a self-help group, whether you are someone with a personal concern or a professional working in the field.

You can phone the Clearinghouse at (973) 625-7101 between 9:00 AM and 5:00 PM, Eastern time. People who use Telecommunication Devices for the Deaf may call (973) 625-9053. You may write them at American Self-Help Clearinghouse, St. Clares-Riverside Medical Center, Denville, NJ 07834. The Self-Help Sourcebook costs $10, plus $2 handling and postage.

Another national referral agency is the National Self-Help Clearinghouse, CUNY Graduate Center, 25 W. 43d St, Room 620, New York, NY 10036. Their phone number is (212) 642-2944.

## Contact the Local or National Service Office

Most groups that have meetings in more than one state have a single address and phone number serving as a national distributor for information. Below are the addresses and phone numbers for several addiction-oriented recovery support groups. These contacts can give you information about local meeting times and places, starting a meeting yourself, or connecting with someone somewhere in the country who can give you guidance and support.

Alcoholics Anonymous World Services, Inc.
475 Riverside Drive, 11th Floor
New York, NY 10115
(212) 870-3400

Atheists in Recovery
2205 22nd Avenue
South Minneapolis, MN 55404
(612) 724-8238

Cocaine Anonymous
3740 Overland Avenue, #H
Los Angeles, CA 90034
(800) 347-8998

Narcotics Anonymous
World Service Office
PO Box 9999
Van Nuys, CA 91409
(818) 773-9999

Rational Recovery Systems
PO Box 800
Lotus, CA 95651
(800) 303-2873

Secular Organizations for Sobriety
5521 Grosvenor Blvd.
Los Angeles, CA 90066
(310) 821-8430

Women for Sobriety
PO Box 618
Quakertown, PA 18951-0618
(800) 333-1606

# Read a Good Book

If you have all the human-to-human support you could use but would still like more support, then check out the many sources of support you can read. Larger bookstores all have sections dedicated to recovery books. Many smaller bookstores will also have a few titles available.

Your local library will have a lot of books on recovery also. If you don't know a particular title you'd like, then check the listings under addiction, alcohol, alcoholism, chemical dependency, drugs, dependency, or recovery and see what you find.

Here are a few titles recommended to help your recovery program:

*The Addiction Workbook*, by Patrick Fanning and John T. O'Neill. This is an excellent resource to help you take stock of the things in your life that need changing, or that you could improve to help you maintain your recovery. The book would be a great source of support to use along with this book, particularly once you get up to goal six. (Published by New Harbinger Publications, Inc.)

*The Recovery Resource Book*, by Barbara Yoder. This book gives a limited overview of the definitions of dependency and recovery for a variety of conditions, not just chemical dependency. It also gives some good ideas about lifestyle change. However, it also contains impressive lists of recovery literature, support groups, and phone support for recovery. (Published by Fireside/Simon and Schuster.)

*Many Roads, One Journey*, by Charlotte Kasl. This book analyzes the Twelve Steps from a feminist perspective. Recovery is defined holistically, taking into account many different aspects of one's life. It's a good resource to get ideas and information for recovery. (Published by Harper Perennial.)

*Alcoholics Anonymous*, published by AA World Services, Inc. This is the granddaddy of recovery books. It gives details of the spiritual program of recovery followed by members of AA. You can find it at any AA meeting, or at some bookstores. A book store could also order it for you. (Published by AA World Services, Inc.)

*Narcotics Anonymous*, published by NA World Service Office, Inc. NA was the second Twelve-Step organization founded. It is the sister spiritual organization to AA, following the same guidelines for recovery. (Published by NA World Service Office, Inc.)

*The Small Book*, by Jack Trimpey. This book was written by the founder of Rational Recovery. The book takes a very critical look at the Twelve Steps and of spirituality, in general. It outlines an intellectual process of recovery which would work for people who would like a brainy approach to recovery. (Published by Delacorte Press.)

*Goodbye Hangovers, Hello Life*, by Jean Kirkpatrick. This book, written by the founder of Women for Sobriety, examines alcoholism from an emotional point of view. Recovery guidelines include raising self-esteem and evaluating one's diet. You may only be able to find this book in a library. (Published by Atheneum.)

# One Last Look

Finally, here are the ten therapeutic goals explained in this book, all together:

**Goal One:** I admit I am unable to always tell how much I will use or drink when I choose to use drugs or alcohol, nor can I always tell what will happen when I choose to use or drink.

**Goal Two:** I name certain people and things besides myself that could help me restore sound judgment to my life.

**Goal Three:** I commit to seek guidance from those sources of support in my day-to-day decision-making.

**Goal Four:** I make a thorough list of those thoughts, attitudes, and behaviors I use to set myself up to relapse, and another list of those thoughts, attitudes, and behaviors I use to keep myself abstinent, then share and revise my lists with at least one of my sources of support.

**Goal Five:** I feel entirely ready to humbly follow the guidance of my sources of support to help me reduce my relapse-prone behavior and improve my chances for abstinence.

**Goal Six:** I write a plan of action to prevent relapse and protect my abstinence, and get ready to put the plan into action.

**Goal Seven:** I put the plan to work (except when to do so would hurt someone more than it would help me).

**Goal Eight:** I evaluate my progress, praising myself as appropriate, and changing my plan when necessary.

**Goal Nine:** I identify and use new sources of support that could help me overcome new problems.

**Goal Ten:** Having made satisfying improvements in sound judgment by using these goals, I continue to make improvements in other areas of my life, as this process has become my basic nature.

This book provides an outline for recovery. The process has been proven to be effective for chemically dependent people, and useful for the professionals who work with them. You can use the process to improve your life by finding the way to avoid relapse, maintain your abstinence, and remain forever drug- or alcohol-free. Remember that the process goes on forever. You're not trying to win a race, you're trying to improve your life. You can do it, and you will if you follow the goals in a paced, but not too fast manner. Good luck as you progress.

# References

Alcoholics Anonymous. 1939. *Alcoholics Anonymous.* New York: Alcoholics Anonymous World Services, Inc.

———. 1980. *Dr. Bob and the Good Oldtimers.* New York: Alcoholics Anonymous World Services, Inc.

———. 1988. *Narcotics Anonymous,* 5th Ed. Van Nuys, Calif.: World Services Office, Inc.

———. 1984. *"Pass It On:" The Story of Bill Wilson and How the AA Message Reached the World.* New York: Alcoholics Anonymous World Services, Inc.

———. 1981. *Twelve Steps and Twelve Traditions.* New York: Alcoholics Anonymous World Services, Inc.

American Psychiatric Association. 1994. *Diagnostic and Statistical Manual of Mental Disorders,* 4th Ed. Washington, D.C.: American Psychiatric Association.

American Society of Addiction Medicine. 1996. *Patient Placement Criteria for the Treatment of Substance-Related Disorders,* 2d Ed.

Chevy Chase, Md.: American Society of Addiction Medicine, Inc.

Booth, P. G. 1990. Maintained controlled drinking following severe alcohol dependence—a case study. *British Journal of Addiction* 85(3):315–22.

Brown, S. 1985. *Treating the Alcoholic: A Developmental Model of Recovery.* New York: John Wiley & Sons.

Bufe, C. 1991. *Alcoholics Anonymous: Cult or Cure?* Tucson, Ariz.: Sharp Press.

Dorris, M. 1989. *The Broken Cord: A Family's Ongoing Struggle with Fetal Alcohol Syndrome.* New York: HarperCollins.

Emery, H. G., and K. G. Brewster, eds. 1938. *The New Century Dictionary of the English Language.* New York: D. Appleton-Century Company.

Fanning, P., and J. T. O'Neill. 1996. *The Addiction Workbook.* Oakland, Calif.: New Harbinger Publications, Inc.

Galanter, M., and P. Buckley. 1978. Evangelical religion and meditation: psychotherapeutic effects. *Journal of Nervous and Mental Disease* 166(10):685–92.

Gorski, T. 1989 *Passages Through Recovery: An Action Plan for Preventing Relapse.* San Francisco: Harper & Row.

Gorski, T. 1986. Relapse prevention planning: a new recovery tool. *Alcohol Health and Research World* 11(1):6–8.

Griffith, E. E. H., T. English, and V. Mayfield. 1980. Possession, prayer and testimony: therapeutic aspects of the Wednesday night meeting in a black church. *Psychiatry* 43(2):120–8.

Harrison, P. A., N. G. Hoffman, and S. G. Steed. 1991. Drug and alcohol addiction treatment outcome. In *Comprehensive Handbook of Drug and Alcohol Addiction,* edited by N. S. Miller. New York: Marcel Dekker, Inc.

International Classification of Diseases, Vol. 10 *Classification of Mental and Behavioral Disorders: Clinical Descriptors and Diagnostic Guidelines.* 1993. Geneva: World Health Organization.

International Classification of Diseases, Vol. 10 *Classification of Mental and Behavioral Disorders: Diagnostic Criteria for Research.* 1993. Geneva: World Health Organization.

Jellineck, E. M. 1960. *The Disease Concept of Alcoholism.* New Brunswick, N.J.: Hillhouse Press.

Johnson, V. E. 1980. *I'll Quit Tomorrow,* Rev. Ed. San Francisco: Harper & Row.

Kasl, C. D. 1992. *Many Roads, One Journey.* New York: Harper Perennial.

Kaster, T., and T. Kaster. 1991. Criteria for diagnosis. In *Comprehensive Handbook of Drug and Alcohol Addiction,* edited by N. S. Miller. New York: Marcel Dekker, Inc.

Kirkpatrick, J. 1986. *Goodbye Hangovers, Hello Life.* New York: Atheneum.

Lemere, F. 1987. Aversion treatment of alcoholism: some reminiscences. *British Journal of Addiction* 82(3):257–8.

McCrady, B. S., and S. Irvine. 1989. Self-help groups. In *Handbook of Alcoholism Treatment Approaches: Effective Alternatives,* edited by R. K. Hester and W. R. Miller. New York: Pergamon Press.

McNeece, C. A. and D. M. Dinitto. 1994. *Chemical Dependency: A systems Approach.* Englewood Cliffs, N.J.: Prentice Hall, Inc.

Mann, G. A. 1991. History and theory of a treatment for drug and alcohol addiction. In *Comprehensive Handbook of Drug and Alcohol Addiction,* edited by N. S. Miller. New York: Marcel Dekker, Inc.

Miller, M., T. Gorski, and D. Miller. 1982. *Learning to Live Again: A Guide for Recovery From Alcoholism.* Independence, Mo.: Independence Press.

Peele, S. 1989. *Diseasing of America: Addiction Treatment Out of Control.* Lexington, Mass.: Lexington Books.

Pendery, M., and J. West. 1982. Controlled drinking by alcoholics? *Science* 217:169–75.

Smith, J. W., and P. J. Frawley. 1990. Long-term abstinence from alcohol in patients receiving aversion therapy as part of a multimodal inpatient program. *Journal of Substance Abuse Treatment* 7:77–82.

Sobell, M. B., and L. C. Sobell. 1987. Stalking white elephants. *British Journal of Addiction* 82(3):245–7.

Sobell, M. B., and L. C. Sobell. 1976. Second-year treatment outcome of alcoholics treated by individualized behavior therapy: results. *Behavioral Research Therapy* 14:195–215.

Stockwell, T. 1986. Cracking an old chestnut: is controlled drinking possible for the person who has been severely alcohol dependent? *British Journal of Addiction* 81(4):455–6.

Trimpey, J. 1992. *The Small Book,* 2d Ed. New York: Delacorte Press/Bantam Doubleday Dell Publishing Group, Inc.

Vaillant, G. 1983. *The Natural History of Alcoholism.* Cambridge, MA: Harvard University Press.

White, B. J., and E. J. Madraf. 1992. *The Self-Help Sourcebook,* 4th Ed. Denville, N.J.: St. Clares-Riverside Medical Center.

Yoder, B. 1990. *The Recovery Resource Book.* New York: Fireside/Simon and Schuster.

Zuska, J. J., and J. A. Pursch. 1988. Long term management. In *Alcoholism: A Practical Treatment Guide,* 2d Ed., edited by S. E. Gitlow and H. S. Peyser. San Diego: Grune and Stratton.

# Some Other New Harbinger Self-Help Titles

*Dr. Carl Robinson's Basic Baby Care*, $10.95
*Better Boundries: Owning and Treasuring Your Life*, $13.95
*Goodbye Good Girl*, $12.95
*Being, Belonging, Doing*, $10.95
*Thoughts & Feelings, Second Edition*, $18.95
*Depression: How It Happens, How It's Healed*, $14.95
*Trust After Trauma*, $13.95
*The Chemotherapy & Radiation Survival Guide, Second Edition*, $13.95
*Heart Therapy*, $13.95
*Surviving Childhood Cancer*, $12.95
*The Headache & Neck Pain Workbook*, $14.95
*Perimenopause*, $13.95
*The Self-Forgiveness Handbook*, $12.95
*A Woman's Guide to Overcoming Sexual Fear and Pain*, $14.95
*Mind Over Malignancy*, $12.95
*Treating Panic Disorder and Agoraphobia*, $44.95
*Scarred Soul*, $13.95
*The Angry Heart*, $13.95
*Don't Take It Personally*, $12.95
*Becoming a Wise Parent For Your Grown Child*, $12.95
*Clear Your Past, Change Your Future*, $12.95
*Preparing for Surgery*, $17.95
*Coming Out Everyday*, $13.95
*Ten Things Every Parent Needs to Know*, $12.95
*The Power of Two*, $12.95
*It's Not OK Anymore*, $13.95
*The Daily Relaxer*, $12.95
*The Body Image Workbook*, $17.95
*Living with ADD*, $17.95
*Taking the Anxiety Out of Taking Tests*, $12.95
*The Taking Charge of Menopause Workbook*, $17.95
*Living with Angina*, $12.95
*Five Weeks to Healing Stress: The Wellness Option*, $17.95
*Choosing to Live: How to Defeat Suicide Through Cognitive Therapy*, $12.95
*Why Children Misbehave and What to Do About It*, $14.95
*When Anger Hurts Your Kids*, $12.95
*The Addiction Workbook*, $17.95
*The Mother's Survival Guide to Recovery*, $12.95
*The Chronic Pain Control Workbook, Second Edition*, $17.95
*Fibromyalgia & Chronic Myofascial Pain Syndrome*, $19.95
*Flying Without Fear*, $12.95
*Kid Cooperation: How to Stop Yelling, Nagging & Pleading and Get Kids to Cooperate*, $12.95
*The Stop Smoking Workbook: Your Guide to Healthy Quitting*, $17.95
*Conquering Carpal Tunnel Syndrome and Other Repetitive Strain Injuries*, $17.95
*Wellness at Work: Building Resilience for Job Stress*, $17.95
*An End to Panic: Breakthrough Techniques for Overcoming Panic Disorder, Second Edition*, $17.95
*Living Without Procrastination: How to Stop Postponing Your Life*, $12.95
*Goodbye Mother, Hello Woman: Reweaving the Daughter Mother Relationship*, $14.95
*Letting Go of Anger: The 10 Most Common Anger Styles and What to Do About Them*, $12.95
*Messages: The Communication Skills Workbook, Second Edition*, $13.95
*Coping With Chronic Fatigue Syndrome: Nine Things You Can Do*, $12.95
*The Anxiety & Phobia Workbook, Second Edition*, $18.95
*The Relaxation & Stress Reduction Workbook, Fourth Edition*, $17.95
*Living Without Depression & Manic Depression: A Workbook for Maintaining Mood Stability*, $17.95
*Coping With Schizophrenia: A Guide For Families*, $13.95
*Visualization for Change, Second Edition*, $13.95
*Postpartum Survival Guide*, $13.95
*Angry All the Time: An Emergency Guide to Anger Control*, $12.95
*Couple Skills: Making Your Relationship Work*, $13.95
*Self-Esteem, Second Edition*, $13.95
*I Can't Get Over It, A Handbook for Trauma Survivors, Second Edition*, $15.95
*Dying of Embarrassment: Help for Social Anxiety and Social Phobia*, $12.95
*The Depression Workbook: Living With Depression and Manic Depression*, $17.95
*Men & Grief: A Guide for Men Surviving the Death of a Loved One*, $13.95
*When the Bough Breaks: A Helping Guide for Parents of Sexually Abused Children*, $11.95
*When Once Is Not Enough: Help for Obsessive Compulsives*, $13.95
*The Three Minute Meditator, Third Edition*, $12.95
*Beyond Grief: A Guide for Recovering from the Death of a Loved One*, $13.95
*Hypnosis for Change: A Manual of Proven Techniques, Third Edition*, $13.95
*When Anger Hurts*, $13.95

Call **toll free, 1-800-748-6273,** to order. Have your Visa or Mastercard number ready. Or send a check for the titles you want to New Harbinger Publications, Inc., 5674 Shattuck Ave., Oakland, CA 94609. Include $3.80 for the first book and 75¢ for each additional book, to cover shipping and handling. (California residents please include appropriate sales tax.) Allow two to five weeks for delivery.
*Prices subject to change without notice.*